A Guide to Tracing Your Sligo Ancestors

Acknowledgements

Many organisations and individuals assisted in the writing of this guide. In particular I would like to acknowledge the following for assistance in accessing records and/or for supplying illustrations:
National Library of Ireland for assistance and for the use of illustrations of their holdings; Patrick Gannon of Sligo Public Library; Adrian Regan, John McTernan and their team at Sligo Heritage and Genealogy Centre; Eileen Hewson of Kabristan Archives; Ross Weldon of www. Findmypast.ie; and National Archives. I would also like to acknowledge the major input of my colleague Brian Smith in the editing and proofing of the text.

A Guide to
Tracing Your Sligo Ancestors

James G. Ryan

FLYLEAF PRESS

First published in 2012

Flyleaf Press
4 Spencer Villas
Glenageary
Co. Dublin
Ireland
www.flyleaf.ie

© 2012 Flyleaf Press

British Library cataloguing in Publications Data available

ISBN 978-1-907990-04-5

Cover Illustration:
Eoin Ryan
www.eoinryanart.com

Layout:
Brian Smith

Contents

Foreword

Sligo is a maritime county in the Province of Connacht, bordered on the west by the Atlantic, on the north by Leitrim and on the east and south by Roscommon and Mayo. In the 19th century, the capital Sligo (population 20,000), was the principal emigration port during the mass exodus that occurred from the north-west of Ireland.

The native Gaelic families in the area are MacDonagh, MacFirbis, O'Connor, O'Dowd, O'Gara and O'Hara. In the aftermath of the Norman invasion they regained possession of their hereditary lands. They were later joined by mercenary families such as MacDonnells, MacSweenys and O'Harts. In the Cromwellian Settlement that followed upon the unsuccessful 1641 Uprising, the aforementioned chieftains forfeited most if not all of their hereditary possessions. Their lands were allotted, in lieu of pay, to the disbanded officers in Coote's Regt. Among these were the ancestors of well-known county families - Cooper, Crofton, Gore, Nicholson, Ormsby, Parke, Phibbs, Irwin and Wood.

In the 'Census' of 1659 the principal surnames in the County were: O'Hart, O'Connor, McGowan and Feeney in Carbury; O'Gara in Coolavin; McDonagh, (O') Scanlon, O'Healy and Brennan in Corran; Gallagher and O'Hara in Leyney; O'Dowd, Kelly, Burke, Boland and McDonnell in Tireragh; McDonagh, Conlon, Breheny, Healy and Higgins in Tirerrill. The most common surnames in the Borough of Sligo in 1749 (Elphin Census) were: Kelly, Gallagher, McGowan, (O)'Hart, Higgins, Connor/O'Connor, McDonagh, Walsh, Egan and (O)'Crean. An index of computerised marriage records in the Sligo Centre (page 154) shows that the most common surnames are: Gallagher, Brennan, McGowan, Kelly, Gilmartin, Healy, Walsh, Hart, Feeney, MacDonagh and Connor /O'Connor.

Sligo has been the birthplace of many individuals who achieved fame or notoriety at home and abroad. These included Duald MacFirbis and Charles O'Conor, noted antiquaries and historians; Charles Phillips and Bourke Cockran, orators of international fame; Ambrose O'Higgins, Governor of Chile and Viceroy of Peru; Count Nicholas Taaffe of the Holy Roman Empire; General Michael Corcoran of the 69th New York Brigade; Francis MacDonagh and Hugh H. MacDermot, legal luminaries; eminent chemists, Bryan and William Higgins; Eva Gore-Booth, poetess; Gabriel Stokes, noted mathematician; Edward J. Cooper, the Markree astronomer; R. T. Henn, Yeatsian scholar, and countless others.

As a board-member of the Co. Sligo Heritage and Genealogy Society I welcome this publication which will be an invaluable tool for all those undertaking research into their Sligo ancestry. The layout and contents are easy to follow and author, Jim Ryan, is to be complimented on the comprehensive nature of the source material on offer. "Tracing your Sligo Ancestors" is not only a welcome addition to other titles in the series but also a valuable source for students wishing to delve into Sligo's chequered past.

John C. McTernan

John C. McTernan

Seal of Sligo Corporatioon 1612

Abbreviations Used

b.	Baptism
c.	circa
Co.	County
CoI	Church of Ireland
d.	death/died
ed.	Editor /edited (by)
GO	Genealogical Office
	(now part of National Library of Ireland)
GRO	General Register Office
IMC	Irish Manuscripts Commission
Ir. Anc.	Irish Ancestor
Ir. Gen.	Irish Genealogist
J. or Jnl.	Journal
J. Gen. Soc. I.	Journal of Genealogical Society of Ireland
JAPMD	Journal of the Association for the
	Preservation of the Memorials of the Dead
LC	Local Custody
Lib.	Library
m. or marr.	marriage/ married
mf.	microfilm/fiche
Ms/Mss	Manuscript/s
NAI	National Archives of Ireland (formerly PRO)
n.d.	not dated
NLI	National Library of Ireland
p./pp.	page/ pages
PRO	Public Record Office
	(now National Archives of Ireland)
Pr.pr.	Privately printed
PRONI	Public Record Office of Northern Ireland
Pub.	published/ publisher
RC	Roman Catholic
RCB(L)	Representative Church Body (Library)
RIA	Royal Irish Academy
JRSAI	Journal of Royal Society of Antiquarians
	in Ireland
SHGC	Sligo Heritage and Genealogical Centre
	(see page 154)

SLC	Family History Library, Salt Lake City (and branches)
Soc.	Society
SOG	Society of Genealogists
TCD	Trinity College Dublin

The counties and provinces of Ireland

Chapter 1   Introduction

Tracing an ancestor requires patience, persistence and a plan. *Patience* - because you will need to consult many different historical sources, and many will contain no information of value; *Persistence*, because unless you keep trying you will not put all of the information together; and a *Plan* because the process is confusing and generates a lot of data which may ultimately prove useless. You must be organised if you are to make sense of the information you find, and be able to access what is useful when it is needed.

There is no magic formula for successful research. However, initial research should be based on the following principles:

- Record as much detail as possible from living relatives. Even dubious information should not be ignored until the true facts are established. The elimination of false information is as much a part of family research as is the confirmation of valid information.

- Construct a pedigree chart so as not to confuse different generations, especially when a personal (Christian) name is very common within a family, as is often the case.

- Work from the known to the unknown, i.e. always try to establish a connection between a known family member and a previous generation, or another potential family member. Many Irish family names are locally common and it is easy to presume a connection that is not real.

Having gathered as much details as possible from your family members and family papers, you should plan to verify and expand this information using the available records and sources. This book is designed to help you do this. The nature, timeframes and locations of the available sources are described in the following chapters. Descriptions of the available sources are arranged by chapter according to the source type, i.e. civil registration, church records, census returns, newspapers, directories etc.

No source will have the full story. Your task is to pick the useful bits that they contain and piece them together to form a comprehensive picture of a family's existence. The final picture depends on the number and quality of these details. Sligo, in common with many western Irish counties, does not have a huge resource of records. Therefore it is important that those available are used effectively.

The records available to you vary widely in their genealogical content and value. They are usually differentiated as **Primary Sources** which record information directly obtained from or about your ancestor (e.g. Civil registration of births, marriages and deaths; church records; census records; Wills and administrations) and **Secondary Sources** which were created for other purposes, but nevertheless assist the researcher to locate an ancestor in an area at a particular time (e.g. Tithe Applotment, Griffith's Valuations, local histories etc). Some of the above sources will also provide the researcher with interesting background details.

Other sources can also be of great assistance in providing information about the lifestyle of an ancestor. They can, in some cases, be used to define a timeframe in which a primary source can be consulted. They include newspapers, journals, published family histories and documents.

For the optimal use of these records, it is important to understand the system of administrative divisions used in Ireland. These divisions or areas are described in Chapter 2. They are vital in determining an ancestor's address or location. Many, if not most, sources are arranged according to such divisions, and an understanding of the different elements of an ancestor's address is therefore important.

The abbreviations used throughout the book are explained on page 8 and contact details for the organisations, libraries and archives cited can be found in Chapter 13. Most publications cited are to be found in most major libraries and archives.

While County Sligo is not as wealthy in genealogical sources as some other counties, the collection of primary, secondary and other sources covered will help provide the researcher with a fascinating insight as to how and where an ancestor lived.

Firstly, some background on this interesting Connaught county. It contains the towns of Sligo, Ballymote, Tubbercurry, Collooney, Ballysodare, and Enniscrone, and was the ancestral territory of a branch of the O'Connors, called O'Connor Sligo. Other Gaelic families associated with the county include O'Dowd, O'Gara, O'Hara, O'Hart, McDonagh, Mac Firbis, and O'Colman. The site of the town of Sligo has been of strategic importance since ancient times as all traffic on the coastal route between South and North had to ford the river here. A fortress which guarded this ford was plundered by Norse pirates as early as A.D. 807.

After the Norman invasion of Connacht in 1235, Sligo was granted to Maurice Fitzgerald who effectively founded Sligo town by building a castle there in 1245 and making it his residence. The Taaffe family was among the Norman families who settled in the county. Further settlers were brought into the county at various periods, including weavers from the north of Ireland brought in by Lord Shelbourne in 1749. The county was, and still is, home to several major family estates, some of whose records are available for research.

Apart from the weaving industry and some mining operations, Sligo was basically an agricultural county. The town of Sligo was an important port in the eighteenth and nineteenth centuries. It was also an important port of emigration, and the main port of emigration for the Northwest of Ireland during Famine times.

The peak of population was reached in 1841 at 181,000. The Great Famine of 1845-47 badly affected the county and the population had dropped by 52,000 in ten years, including some 20,000 deaths. By 1901 the population had fallen to 84,000 and is currently 56,000. Its most notable sons are arguably the poet William Butler Yeats and his painter brother Jack B. Yeats.

The county of Sligo is distributed into six baronies and thirty-nine parishes.

The baronies are Carbury, Tyrerah, Tyrerril, Corran, Liney, and Coolavin.

The barony of *Carbury*, from between Ballysadare and Sligo down to the sea, forms the northern extremity of the county; it is thirteen miles long, by about nine broad, bounded on the east by Leitrim, on the north and west by the sea, and on the south by the baronies of Tyrerril and Liney. Those two baronies, after running parallel with each other a couple of miles southward, receive and inclose between them the barony of *Corran;* then the whole three proceed southward together, and constitute the greatest and best part of the county, the barony of Tyrerril sketching along side of Leitrim, which is on the east, and Corran on the west to Roscommon county. Corran, as mentioned, is included between Tyrerril east and Liney west, and runs south to the barony of Coolavin, by which it is there bounded; and away this barony of Coolavin runs south-east from Corran, and from the main body of Sligo, among the counties of Roscommon and Mayo; by the former it is bounded on the east and south, by Mayo on the west. The barony of Tyrera runs upwards of twenty miles away from

An extract from
'Statistical Survey of the county of Sligo'
by James McParlan M.D. (Dublin 1802)

Chapter 2

Administrative Divisions and Maps

Both the state and the church have administrative needs which required dividing the county into geographical areas. It is important to understand these areas and their relationship when locating the records. You should also expect some variations in the spelling of the place-names which are found in the records. This is a result of the gradual transformation of Gaelic place-names into English by different sets of administrators. The divisions you will come across are as follows:

Civil Divisions

Townland
The townland is the smallest civil division within a county. It is an ancient division of land which is highly variable in size, from 10 acres to several thousand. There are 1,325 townlands in Sligo; they are the most specific part of an ancestor's address in rural areas. Sligo Library have an on-line system which will find all townlands and provide access to detailed maps of each – see Online map collection at the end of this chapter.

Civil Parish
There are 41 civil parishes in Sligo; each is formed of many townlands. (See map on page 22). It should be noted that the boundaries of some civil parishes cross barony and county boundaries. In some cases civil parishes are divided into unconnected parts, for example the civil parish of Kilcolman is partly in the barony of Clanmorris and partly in the barony of Costello. Likewise, the parish of Kilcommon can be found in the northern barony of Erris and in the southern barony of Kilmaine. Many civil parishes make up a barony.

Barony

The barony is generally based on the ancient 'tuath' or territory of an Irish clan. There are 273 baronies in Ireland which appear mainly in land records. The six baronies in County Sligo are Carbury, Tireragh, Leyny, Corran, Tirerril and Coolavin.

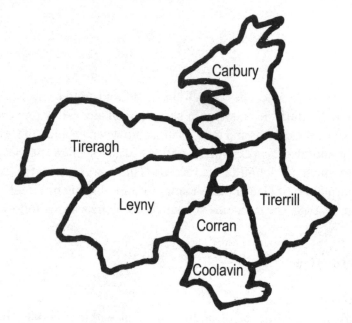

The baronies of County Sligo

Poor Law Union

The Poor Law Union (PLU) was established under the Poor Law Act of 1838 for use in the administration of distress relief and the upkeep of the poor and destitute. They are unrelated to any other older division and do not adhere to barony or county boundaries. Each is based around (and named from) a major town. Sligo has five major PLUs: Sligo, Dromore West, Tobercurry and Boyle, and parts of two parishes are in Ballina PLU (which mainly covers County Mayo). These Poor Law Unions later became used for other local admistrative purposes, such as elections and in the civil registration of births, marriages and deaths. See http://www.workhouses.org.uk/Sligo/ also see page 27.

The poor law unions of County Sligo

District Electoral Division

The District Electoral Division (DED) is a sub-division of the Poor Law Union, in which information for the official censuses of Ireland is compiled and arranged. It was also used for the elections of local and national representatives, under the Local Government Act of 1898.

Ecclesiastical Divisions

Church of Ireland Parish

The Ecclesiastical Divisions used by the Church of Ireland (CoI) had a specific significance for record purposes. Until the late 19th century, the Church of Ireland was also the 'Established Church' or state church. In this capacity it performed several functions which are now performed by the state. These include Probate (proving of wills) and the granting of marriage and some other forms of licence. Church of Ireland divisions therefore have particular relevance when searching certain record types. While generally conforming to civil parish boundaries, some Church of Ireland churches may serve several civil parishes. This is particularly so in Sligo where the Church of Ireland community was always small.

Catholic Church Parish

Although Catholic Church parish boundaries were identical to those of the Church of Ireland until the Reformation, the practical process of parish management caused changes to parish boundaries. Catholic parishes now rarely conform exactly to civil parish boundaries, although in most cases the difference is small. They may, however, have the same name as the civil parish in which they are located.

Other denominations have their own forms of administrative organisation, usually not based on a formal geographical area. A full account of these administrations is given in 'Irish Church Records' (Flyleaf Press 2001).

Useful Guides to Administrative Divisions

To establish the divisions which make up an ancestor's 'genealogical address' the following references are the most commonly available.

1655-59. Index of Parishes and Townlands of Ireland

This is mainly useful in understanding the extent and location of parishes in older record sources. It was compiled and edited by Yann Goblet, based on areas mentioned in Sir. William Petty's Manuscript Barony Maps. It was published by the IMC (Dublin 1932).

1837. Lewis's Topographical Dictionary of Ireland

This three volume set contains an alphabetically arranged account of all civil parishes, major market towns, post towns, seaports, islands and many villages. For each it provides a brief historical account, social and economic conditions, and major landowners. The divisions of the religious denominations are described. A set of 32 maps accompany this edition. These maps have been republished in several sources. This source is widely available in libraries, it is also available on CD at www.archivecdbooks.ie. see page example on page 19.

1838. Ordnance Survey Field Name Books

The Ordnance Survey Office (OS) is the official mapmaker (cartographer) in Ireland (see www.osi.ie). The field name books are the notebooks used by surveyors compiling the first Ordnance Survey maps of Sligo in 1838. They are arranged by civil parish and list each townland alphabetically. Although varying slightly between areas, the details usually include: townland name in Irish and English; derivation

BALLYMOTE, a market and post-town, in the parish of EMLYFAD, barony of CORRAN, county of SLIGO, and province of CONNAUGHT, 11 miles (S. by W.) from Sligo, and 94½ miles (W. N. W.) from Dublin; containing 875 inhabitants. This place appears to have derived its origin from a castle built in 1300 by Richard de Burgo, Earl of Ulster, which, after its seizure by the native Irish during the insurrection of 1641, was found to be of such strength as to offer a serious obstacle to the complete subjugation of Connaught; it was at length taken, in 1652, by the united forces of Ireton and Sir C. Coote. A small monastery for Franciscan friars of the third order was founded here by the sept of Mac Donogh, and at the suppression was granted to Sir H. Broncard, who assigned it to Sir W. Taaffe, Knt. : an inquisition of the 27th of Elizabeth records that it belonged to the castle, and had been totally destroyed by the insurgents. The town is situated at the junction of six roads, but has not one principal road passing through it : it consists of one main street, and contains 140 houses. The surrounding country is well cultivated, and its surface agreeably undulates; and there is a good view from an obelisk erected by Lady Arabella Denny on a small hill near the town. In the immediate vicinity is Earl's Field, the property of Sir R. Gore Booth, Bart., to whom the town belongs; and in a delightful situation, within a quarter of a mile, is the glebe-house, which commands a fine prospect of the surrounding mountains and the distant hill of Knocknaree. About 2½ miles from the town is Temple House, the handsome residence of Col. A. Perceval, beautifully situated on the banks of a lake of that name, and in a fine demesne containing some good old timber; on the edge of the lake are the ruins of the old house, which was built by the O'Hara family in 1303, and was afterwards given to the Knights Hospitallers. The linen manufacture was formerly carried on here to a great extent, under the encouragement of the Rt. Hon. Thos. Fitz~~~~~~~~~~~~~~~~~~~~~~~ extinct. The ~~~~~~

An extract from
'A Topographical Dictionary of Ireland' by Samuel Lewis (London 1837)
- see page 18

of name; Proprietor's name; and other comments. The original transcripts are in the NLI where typescripts are also held.

1844-45. Parliamentary Gazetteer of Ireland
This is similar to Lewis's Topographical Dictionary of Ireland in content and arrangement. It was published in three volumes: Vol.I. A – C (1845), Vol.II. D – M (1845), Vol.III. N – Z with index included (1846). Reference: NLI. Ir.9141 p30.

1851. Townland Index of Ireland
This provides a full alphabetical listing of all townlands, towns, civil parishes and baronies of Ireland giving their location, area and map reference. For each townland the relevant County, Barony, Civil Parish and Poor Law Union is provided. It was published as an aid for officials compiling the 1851 census. It was originally published by Thom's as 'An Index to the Townlands and Towns, Parishes and Baronies of Ireland'. It is widely available in libraries. Similar volumes were published for the censuses of 1841, 1861, 1871 etc. The spelling and occurrence of some townlands varied between censuses so it may occasionally be useful to consult some of these, see page 21.

1885. Townlands in Poor Law Unions
If you know the name of a townland, it can sometimes be useful to establish the names of surrounding townlands. This book lists the townlands within each Poor Law Union, and by Civil Parish within each PLU. It is also useful to establish the spelling of townland names. Compiled by George B. Handran, from 'Lists of Townlands in Poor Law Unions' dated 1885 and later. It was published by Higginson (USA, 1997).

Sligo Library Online Map Collection
Sligo County Library has created an excellent interactive and user-friendly map website, which allows users to explore every townland in the county. It contains digitised versions of all 1837 Ordnance Survey maps (6-inch), and also the 1659 Down Survey Maps. It runs on MapBrowser software which is compatible with the majority of browsers. It will allow detailed review of the features of every townland, and also provides a way of finding the location of each townland within the county. It is difficult to find from the library home-page, but can be accessed at: www.sligolibrary.ie/sligolibrarynew/LocalStudies

No. of Sheet of the Ordnance Survey Maps.	Townlands and Towns.	Area in Statute Acres. A. R. P.	County.	Barony.	Parish.	Poor Law Union in 1857.	Townland Census of 1851, Part I. Vol.	Page
25, 32	Carrownloughan	512 1 5	Sligo	Leyny	Killoran	Tobercurry	IV.	230
93	Carrownluggaun	45 3 2	Mayo	Costello	Bekan	Claremorris	IV.	139
48	Carrownolan	277 0 21	Roscommon	Athlone	Kiltoom	Athlone	IV.	183
3	Carrownoona	423 1 25	Leitrim	Rosclogher	Rossinver	Ballyshannon	IV.	111
21	Carrownphull	83 2 35	Longford	Rathcline	Rathcline	Longford	I.	164
59, 67	Carrownreddy	297 3 37a	Tipperary, S.R.	Clanwilliam	Tipperary	Tipperary	II.	312
26	Carrownree	413 2 17b	Sligo	Corran	Emlaghfad	Sligo	IV.	226
13, 19	Carrownree	297 3 2	Sligo	Tireragh	Skreen	Dromore West	IV.	235
28	Carrownrinny	70 0 25	Roscommon	Roscommon	Kilcooley	Strokestown	IV.	210
28	Carrownrinny	70 2 7	Roscommon	Roscommon	Killukin	Strokestown	IV.	210
11	Carrownrod	489 2 11	Sligo	Tireragh	Easky	Dromore West	IV.	233
57	Carrownrooaun	134 1 25	Galway	Clare	Annaghdown	Tuam	IV.	16
11	Carrownrush	322 3 27	Sligo	Tireragh	Easky	Dromore West	IV.	233
12	Carrownrush	148 1 30	Sligo	Tireragh	Kilmacshalgan	Dromore West	IV.	234
119	Carrownskehaun	241 1 18	Mayo	Clanmorris	Crossboyne	Claremorris	IV.	132
23, 24	Carrownskeheen	207 0 38	Roscommon	Ballintober North	Kilglass	Strokestown	IV.	186
27	Carrownspurraun	475 3 2	Sligo	Tirerrill	Kilraacallan	Sligo	IV.	239
17, 30	Carrowntanlis	249 0 32c	Galway	Dunmore	Tuam	Tuam	IV.	35
47	Carrowntarriff	454 1 17d	Roscommon	Athlone	Taghboy	Athlone	IV.	184
24	Carrowntassona	174 2 5	Waterford	Decies without Drum	Ballylaneen	Kilmacthomas	II.	354
32	Carrowntawa	170 0 14	Sligo	Leyny	Achonry	Tobercurry	IV.	229
25, 33	Carrowntawy	233 3 2	Sligo	Leyny	Kilvarnet	Tobercurry	IV.	232
13	Carrownteane	88 0 26	Sligo	Tireragh	Skreen	Dromore West	IV.	235
23	Carrowntedaun	433 3 8	Clare	Corcomroe	Kilmanaheen	Ennistimon	II.	21
80	Carrownteeaun	314 3 9	Mayo	Gallen	Killedan	Swineford	IV.	150

A page from *'An Index to the Townlands and Towns, Parishes and Baronies of Ireland'* - see page 20

Map of the Civil Parishes of County Sligo

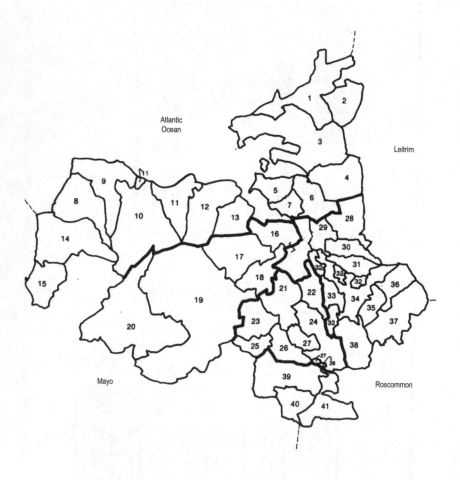

⌐ = Civil parishes adjoining across
    barony boundaries

The Civil Parishes of County Sligo in Alphabetical Order

Map No.	Civil Parish	Map No.	Civil Parish	Map No.	Civil Parish
19	Achonry	21	Emlaghfad	15	Kilmoremoy
38	Aghanagh	40	Kilcolman	22	Kilmorgan
1	Ahamlish	39	Kilfree	29	Kilross
31	Ballynakill	8	Kilglass	26	Kilshalvy
16	Ballysadare	35	Killadoon	25	Kilturra
30	Ballysumaghan	41	Killaraght	18	Kilvarnet
4	Calry	5	Killaspugbrone	2	Rossinver
14	Castleconor	28	Killerry	36	Shancough
23	Cloonoghil	17	Killoran	12	Skreen
13	Dromard	34	Kilmacallan	6	St. John's
3	Drumcliff	7	Kilmacowen	33	Tawnagh
32	Drumcolumb	10	Kilmacshalgan	11	Templeboy
27	Drumrat	20	Kilmacteige	24	Toomour
9	Easky	37	Kilmactranny		

The Civil Parishes of County Sligo in Map number Order

Map No.	Civil parish	Other name or spelling
1	Ahamlish	Ahamplish
2	Rossinver	-
3	Drumcliff	Drumcliffe
4	Calry	Colry
5	Killaspugbrone	Killaspickbrown, Killaspeckbrone
6	St. John's	-
7	Kilmacowen	Kilmacoen
8	Kilglass	-
9	Easky	Easkey
10	Kilmacshalgan	-
11	Templeboy (2 pts)	-
12	Skreen	Skrine
13	Dromard	-
14	Castleconor	-
15	Kilmoremoy	-
16	Ballysadare	Ballysadere, Ballasodare
17	Killoran	-
18	Kilvarnet	-
19	Achonry	Achad, Achad-Conair, Achad-Chaoin
20	Kilmacteige	Kilmacteigue
21	Emlaghfad	Emlyfadd
22	Kilmorgan	-
23	Cloonoghil	Clonymeaghan
24	Toomour	Tumore

25	Kilturra	Kiltora, Kilturragh
26	Kilshalvy (2 pts)	Kilshalvee, Killowshalway
27	Drumrat (2 pts)	Drumratt
28	Killerry	Killery
29	Kilross	Kilrasse
30	Ballysumaghan	-
31	Ballynakill	-
32	Drumcolumb (4 pts)	Drumcollum
33	Tawnagh	Taunagh
34	Kilmacallan	Kilmacallane, Kilmacallen
35	Killadoon	-
36	Shancough	Shancoe
37	Kilmactranny	Kilmactrany
38	Aghanagh	Aughanagh
39	Kilfree	-
40	Kilcolman	Kilcoleman
41	Killaraght	-

Geographically separated civil parishes

In some cases, civil parishes are separated into several geographical parts. In Sligo this occcurs in the civil parishes of Drumcolumb (4 parts), Drumrat (2 parts), Kilshalvy (2 parts) and Templeboy (2 parts).

Name and Registration District.	Vol.	Page
KILLORAN, Maria. Tobercurry	4	456
—— Thomas. Tobercurry	4	452
KILLOUGH, Margaret Jane. Ballymoney	1	148
—— Sarah Morton. Ballymoney	1	138
—— Thomas. Ballymena	1	87
KILLOW, Margaret. Lurgan	1	665
KILMARTIN, Bernard. Dromore West	4	199
—— Bridget. Dromore West	4	197
—— Bridget. Parsonstown	3	513
—— Catherine. Sligo	2	293
—— John. Killala	4	298
—— Martin. Clifden	4	182
—— Mary Bidelia. Sligo	2	293
—— Michael. Ennis	4	205
—— Teresa. Parsonstown	3	520
—— Thomas. Sligo	2	295
KILMURRAY, Rebecca Marv. Dublin, North	2	465
KILPATRICK, Elizabeth. Dublin, North	2	550
—— Marian Teresa. Dublin, North	2	540
—— Samuel. Lurgan	1	674
—— Samuel. Ballymoney	1	145
—— Sarah. Lisburn	1	617
—— William Thomas. Banbridge	1	177
KILROE, Mary. Parsonstown	3	511
KILROY, Anne. Cavan	3	100
—— Bridget. Newport	4	360
—— Bridget. Tobercurry	4	444
—— Bridget. Tobercurry	4	444
—— Catherine. Athlone	3	14
—— Celia. Dromore West	4	193
—— Dominick. Newport	4	362
—— Eliza. Carlow	3	367
—— Fanny. Cavan	3	79
—— Isabella Jane. Skibbereen	5	536
—— Jane. Dromore West	4	194
—— John. Loughrea	4	337
—— Michael. Tobercurry	4	442
—— Michael. Newport	4	362
—— Patrick Bernard. Dublin, North	2	576
KILTY, Patrick. Mallow	5	478
KIMBLAY, Frances Amy. Dublin, South	2	597
KIMMETT, Ellen. Sligo	2	295
KINADAY, Robert. Banbridge	1	183
——————. Florence Annie. Lisburn	1	606

Extract from the
General Registers Office index
to births registered in the July to September quarter of 1880

Chapter 3   Civil Registration

One of the largest and most valuable sources is the Civil Register of births, marriages and deaths, i.e. the official state process for recording these events. Although civil registration began in 1845, only non-Catholic marriages were recorded for the initial period. It was not until 1864 that all marriages, births and deaths were registered. The registers are held by the General Register Office (GRO – see page 149) and the details provided are as follows:

Births

All births from 1st January 1864, specifying: child's name; date and place of birth; name and occupation of father; name and maiden name of mother; name of informant (i.e. the person that registered the birth). - see sample page 28.

Marriages

Non-Catholic marriages from 1st January 1845 and all marriages from 1st January 1864, specifying: place and date of marriage; name, age, address and occupation of bride and groom; name and occupation of the fathers of bride and groom, and witnesses to the marriage. - see sample page 29.

Deaths

All deaths registered from 1st January 1864, specifying: name of deceased; date and place of death; marital status, age, occupation; cause of death; details of informant.

No. (1.)	Date and Place of Birth (2.)	Name (if any) (3.)	Sex. (4.)	Name and Surname and Dwelling-place of Father (5.)	Name and Surname and Maiden Surname of Mother (6.)	Rank or Profession of Father (7.)	Signature, Qualification, and Residence of Informant (8.)	When Registered (9.)	Signature of Registrar (10.)	Baptismal Name if added after Registration of Birth, and Date (11.)
343	18-90 Twenty fifth May Eskragh	John Joseph	M.	Thomas Stenson. Eskragh. Kilmartin.	Ellen. M. Stenson. formerly	Farmer.	her Ellen M. Stenson mark mother. Eskragh.	Twenty Second August 18 90	Gunning Jas? Registrar.	

Superintendent Registrar's District Tobercurry.

Registrar's District Achare.

BIRTHS Registered in the District of Achare **in the Union of** Tobercurry **in the County of** Sligo.

An entry from the *civil register of births* for John Joseph Stenson of Eskragh

- see page 27

No. (1.)	When Married. (2.)	Name and Surname. (3.)	Age. (4.)	Condition. (5.)	Rank or Profession. (6.)	Residence at the Time of Marriage. (7.)	Father's Name and Surname. (8.)	Rank or Profession of Father. (9.)
2	25/2/91	James Flanagan	34	Bachelor	Farmer	Store	James Flanagan	Farmer
		Kate Gilmartin	28	Spinster		Ballindooly	James Gilmartin	

18__ Marriage solemnized at the Roman Catholic Chapel of Ballindooly in the Registrar's District of Calloorey in the Union of Sligo in the County of Sligo

Married in the Roman Catholic Chapel of Ballindooly according to the Rites and Ceremonies of the Roman Catholic Church by me, M. Kelly C.C.

This Marriage was solemnized between us, { James Flanagan / Kate Gilmartin } in the presence of us, { Val. Flanagan / Mary O'Donnell }

An entry from the *civil register of marriages* for the marriage of James Flanagan and Kate Gilmartin

- see page 27

Other civil registration records held by the GRO are:

Births at Sea

Details of Irish subjects whose births took place at sea from 1864. From 1866 a separate index can be found at the back of the main index volume for the relevant year of registration.

Deaths at Sea

Irish subjects whose deaths took place at sea from 1864. From 1866 a separate index can be found at the back of the main index volume for the relevant year of registration.

British Army Service

The civil registers also include the details of births, marriages and deaths of Irish subjects serving with the British Army from 1880. From 1888 a separate index can be found at the back of the main index volumes of the above events.

Births Abroad

From 1864 the birth of Irish subjects abroad had to be notified to the relevant British consul abroad. No index is available but the registers may be inspected at the GRO.

Accessing GRO Records

The original GRO records are held in the GRO headquarters in Roscommon and copies of certificates are provided by post only. Researchers can request a certificate if the exact date and names are known. The GRO will also conduct a search within a five year period for an event. If no date or name is known, there is a research room in Dublin (see page 149) in which the indexes can be searched. Researchers can pay a daily research fee, or a smaller fee to view five consecutive years of indexes. These are alphabetically arranged by surname followed by the forename, registration district, volume number and page number. In the case of deaths index, the age given at the time of death is also included in brackets. When an entry of interest is identified in an index, a photocopy a full certificate can then be obtained. Some of the commercial websites (e.g. ancestry) have indexed all GRO records and will provide volume and page numbers.

Up to 1877 the indexes are in single A to Z yearly volumes. From 1878 each yearly volume is subdivided into quarters, note that the indexes are compiled from the dates of registration and not the date when a birth, marriage or death took place. Therefore the birth of a child in March may appear in the January to March quarter or in the April to June quarter. Likewise a death taking place in December may appear in the October to December quarter or in the first quarter of the following year. Late registrations (which are common) are indexed at the end of each volume.

There are several forms of certificate available. The least expensive is a photocopy of the register (but note that they are not copies from the original register and will not show original signatures or handwriting). Also available are official certified transcripts from the records in short form (basic information only) or long form. The latter are necessary for official use (passport applications etc) but do not contain additional information.

Registration Districts for Sligo

Superintendent Registrar's Districts were used in collating GRO records. The five districts for the county are Sligo, Dromore West, Tobercurry, Boyle and Ballina. Note that the latter two are centred in neighbouring counties. Ballina district, for instance, mainly covers Mayo, while Boyle mainly covers Roscommon. The Superintendent Registrar's District is geographically identical to the Poor Law Union (see PLU map on page 17), so the 'Townland Index' (see pages 20 and 21) can be used to identify the registration district for any townland or parish of interest.

Civil Registration Indexes available elsewhere

A microfilm copy of the indexes to the civil registration of births, marriages and deaths is held at the Dublin City Library and Archive. The index to births for the years 1864, 1865 and 1866 are also available in hard copy in the NLI. (ref LB Thom 3121). County Sligo Heritage and Genealogy Centre (see page 154) also holds copies of civil registrations from 1864 to 1900 for some districts and will conduct searches for a fee.

Civil Registration Indexes On-Line

The site https://wiki.familysearch.org/en/Ireland_Civil_Registration contains additional information and tips on civil registration. This website also includes links to indexes of births, marriages and deaths, providing references for obtaining copies of registration from the GRO. ancestry.com and ancestry.co.uk also indexes GRO records.

International Genealogical Index (IGI)

The IGI is compiled by the Church of Jesus Christ of Latter Day Saints and includes some civil registration details up to about 1867. They can be searched on-line at www.familysearch.org

Deceased Seamen 1887 - 1949

Names of seamen whose deaths were reported to the GRO specifying: name of deceased; age; rank or occupation; official number; name and type of ship; port of registry; cause place and date of death. From 1893 it includes sex; nationality or place of birth, and last place of abode. The source is available in the NLI and the reference is 31242 d.

Chapter 4   Censuses and Census Substitutes

This chapter outlines the official government censuses, and also an extensive list of 'census substitutes', which are sources which list people residing in Sligo at a particular period, with varying additional information. Some of these will only contain names, and may serve only to show that a person of a particular name lived in the county at a particular time. However, most will show some other information which will serve to broaden your information.

Official Government Censuses of Ireland have been carried out at 10 year intervals since 1821. However, the individual household returns for the years 1821-1851 were destroyed in a fire in the Public Record Office in 1921. Returns for the years 1861-1871 were destroyed by Government order to protect confidentiality, and the 1881 and 1891 returns were pulped during the First World War due to a shortage of paper. The National Archives of Ireland site www.nationalarchives. ie provides free on-line access to all of the returns for the 1901 and 1911 censuses. The search capabilities and quality of reproduction of the original returns is excellent and this is a very significant resource for family research. Even those whose ancestors may have left Ireland decades earlier can benefit from the information in these censuses. Many emigrants left family behind in Ireland and the details on this site can provide information on marriage dates of parents. The returns are also available for inspection on microfilm in the National Archives itself. See page 149.

Below is a chronologically arranged list of sources, with a description, and where each can be accessed. These vary significantly in the detail they offer. Some, particularly Voters lists, will only provide a name often without even a parish address. In others the additional detail relates only to their land-holding or rent. However, there are other sources which list occupations, specific addresses and other information and also the basis for further research. Note that some sources which cover a wide period of years (e.g. some directories, estate papers etc.) will also be listed in other chapters, also that some are manuscript sources which may only be available in one archive.

1632   Strafford Survey.
A transcript of the Strafford Survey of Co. Sligo, 1632, with alphabetical list of landed proprietors, and tenants, clergy and others. NLI Ms. 2166. A description of the source is in J. Historical and Archaeological Association of Ireland, Ser. 4, Vol. VI, pt. 1, pp. 176-177, 1883.

1633-36 Rentals of Estates in Sligo.
Rentals of the estates of landed proprietors of the county of Sligo published in *'History of Sligo County and Town from the Accession of James I to the Revolution of 1688'* by W.G. Wood-Martin (Dublin 1889) p.141-193 see page 142.

1641   Books of Survey and Distribution.
Lists the owners of the land in 1640, and the owners following its confiscation and redistribution in 1641. RIA Ms 1 VI. 1; Published by Irish Manuscripts Commission (Dublin 1956).

1641   Protestant Depositions.
Transcripts and images of 8,000 depositions from Protestant men and women of all classes regarding their experiences during the rebellion by the Catholic Irish in October, 1641. A fully searchable digital edition is available at Trinity College Dublin Library http://1641.tcd.ie/

1654-58. The Transplantation to Connaught.
This is arranged by county, subdivided by Barony. It lists planters, their original county and address, and holding. Also local transplantation giving name and original parish address. Irish Manuscripts Commission (Dublin 1970).

WILLIAM HARRISON, Esq.

PARISH OF DRUMRAT.—Clonesanvalle, 1 qr.; . . . had from Brian Oge Mac Donnogh's Father in the behalfe of Capteyne John Baxter his bond, which quarter he soulde to Wm. Harrison . . . it hath good turffe and fire-wood; . . . worth £10 per ann.

GAROD BAXTER.

BARONY OF CARBURY, PARISH OF KILLASPUGBRONE.—Laresse, 1 quar.; one half of it the inheritance of Garod Baxter, whoe settes it to under-tenants for £ . . per annum, 4 barrells of malte, 4 fatt muttons, 8 medders of butter, 12 medders of meale, 20 workmen. The other ½ qr. the inheritance of Hugh Mac Owen Mac Gilleduffe; it is all good arrable lande, it hath 12 dayes mowinge, it will grase 80 cowes, and it is worth £20 per annum. Carownohince, 1 qr.; . . . sett to under-tennants for £18 per annum. It is goode arrable lande uppon the sea betwixt the Ross and Larisse. It will grase 80 cowes, and it is worth £20 per ann.

EDWARD ORMSBY.

BARONY OF TIRERRILL, PARISH OF TAWNAGH.—Cloonegad and Cloonemachin, 1 qr.; . . . bought from Tirlogh Roe Mac Donnogh of Bricke, about 12 years agoe; . . . worth £15 15s. per annum.

JOHN NOLAN, Esq.

BARONY OF TIRERAGH, PARISH OF KILGLASS.—Carowedin, 1 qr.; Carowincoller; Carowconny, 1 qr.; . . . ech qr. sett for £10 per annum. It is all good arrable lande, it hath some turffe, it will grase 120 cowes, and is worth £30 per annum. Iskerowne,[1] 4 qrs.; . . . ech qr. of them sett for £12 per annum, and 4 medders of butter, 8 medders of meale, 4 barrells of malt, 48 workmen. It is all good arrable lande, it hath good turffe; ech qr. of them will grase 50 cowes, and is worth some £15 per annum.

PARISH OF CASTLECONOR.—Ballevoghene, 1 qr.; Carownorlar, 1 qr.; Carowvallyman, 1 qr.; . . . sett . . . to undertennants; . . . worth £43 per ann.

Extract from
Rentals of the estates of landed proprietors, 1633-36
see page 34

1659 **"Census" of Ireland.**
63 landholders in 'Slegoe' county. Edited by S. Pender. Dublin: Stationery Office, 1939.

1664 **Dispossessed Land Owners.**
Article on land owners who lost their land during the Cromwellian settlements. Includes a list of 30 individuals from Sligo. Ir. Gen. Vol.4 No.4 (1971) pp.275 - 302

1665 **Hearth Money Rolls.**
Approx 1300 heads of household, by townland and parish. Anal. Hib. 24 (1967) pp.1-89. Available on several websites e.g. www.failteromhat.com/sligohearth.php. A hand-written copy of this source is also available in NLI Ms 2165. see page 37.

1682 **Rental of the Strafford Estate in Co. Sligo**
Rental of the estate of Earl of Strafford, Madam Margaret Trapps and Mr. Josue Wilson. Lists 201 tenants in Sligo town and 92 outside the town. NLI Ms. 10,223

1689 **Loyalists attainted by James II.**
A list of 64 gentry and clergy (name, residence and occupation) who were attainted (legally deprived of all rights) by James II for their loyalty to William II. Listed in W.G. Wood-Martin 'Sligo and the Enniskilleners' Dublin 1880.

1699 **Jacobite Outlaws.**
69 names (and townland addresses) of landholders named as being outlawed as Jacobites (followers of James II). Anal Hib. 22 (1960) 11-230

1720 **Church of Ireland parishioners of Ballysadare.**
Petition of 45 Church of Ireland parishioners of Ballysadare. Names only. Listed in pp.121-122 of O'Rorke, T. History and antiquities of Ballisodare and Kilvarnet. Dublin 1878. See page 60

1727 **Cooloney Residents.**
25 persons and holdings 'given as residing in Cooloney in 1727' Listed (143-144) in O'Rorke, T. History and antiquities of Ballisodare and Kilvarnet. Dublin 1878 See page 141.

42

Killm bridge

Thomas Povey for two hearths	2.s
Edward Forett for one hearth	2.s
Thomas Plunkett for one hearth	2.s
Hugh Teige for one hearth	2.s
Symon Welsh for one hearth	2.s
Laurence Mogredge for one hearth	2.s
John Tanner for one hearth	2.s
Robert Barrett for one hearth	2.s
William Allen for one hearth	2.s
Francis Boulter for one hearth	2.s
Teige Horane for one hearth	2.s
Laughlin hellan for one hearth	2.s

Ballisumaghan parish

Levally

Brian Roirke for one hearth	2.s
Dermott Heally for one hearth	2.s
John mc Keene for one hearth	2.s
Farrell mc Kelly for one hearth	2.s

Ballisumaghan

Manus mc Keene for one hearth	2.s
Donnell mc Gilleroe for one hearth	2.s
Hugh Hart for one hearth	2.s
Donell mc Keene for one hearth	2.s
John Rily for one hearth	2.s
Thomas Boyde for one hearth	2.s
Laurence Faele for one hearth	2.s

A page from a handwritten copy of the *Hearth Money Rolls of 1665.*
see page 36

1737-68. Estate Papers of Owen Wynne.
Rentals and expense books, 1737-68, major tenants only; covering townlands in the civil parishes of Ahamlish, Ballysadare, Calry, Drumcliff, Killoran, St John's, Tawnagh, Templeboy. NLI MSS.5780-5782;

1737-1768 Account books of Wynne Estate.
3 Ledgers with cash payments to suppliers and workers, and rent receipts from tenants, between 1737 and 1768. Only gives names (and details of services for some suppliers). NLI Ms 5780, 5781 and 5782.

1738-49 Tenants on Wynne Estate.
General accounts books showing receipts from 162 tenants (in Calry and Drumcliffe parishes, and Sligo town) and payments to suppliers. Names, townlands and amounts only. NLI Ms. 5830

1738-53. Estate Papers of Owen Wynne.
Rent ledgers, 1738-53, List of 118 major tenants, indexed; covering townlands in the civil parishes of Ahamlish, Ballysadare, Calry, Drumcliff, Killoran, St John's, Tawnagh, Templeboy. (see also 1768) NLI MSS. 5830-1

1745   Declaration of allegiance to the King
Declaration of allegiance to the King from Owen Wynne, High Sheriff of Sligo, signed by 75 other persons, mainly large land-owners. NLI D 13,111

1749   Religious Census of Elphin Diocese.
This census lists householders, occupation, religion, numbers of children and servant in the Parishes of Aghanagh, Ahamlish, Ballynakill, Ballysumaghan, Drumcliff, Drumcolumb, Killadoon, Kilmacallan, Kilmactranny, Kilross, Shancough, Sligo, and Tawnagh. NAI 2466; NLI n542, p923; available on-line at www.rootsweb.ancestry.com/~irlsli/sligocountyireland.html and on www.findmypast.ie

1753-56 Killoran Tenants of Charles O'Hara.
Six Rental books with 42 tenants and rent details in Killoran parish. NLI 36,318/11 see page 39

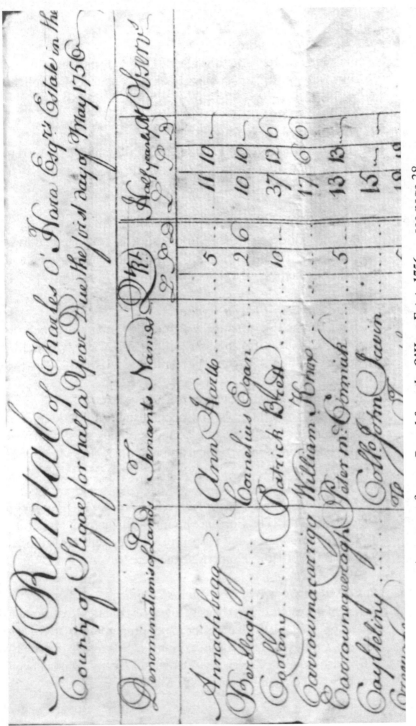

Denominations of Lands	Tenants Names	Yr.	Half-years Rent
		£ s d	£ s d
Anraghbegg	Ann Harte	5 —	11 10 —
Borthagh	Cornelius Egan	2 6	10 10 —
Cootany	Patrick Breen	10 —	37 12 6
Carrowmacarrigg	William Horne		17 6 6
Carrownoveeragh	Peter mc.Donnah	5 —	13 13 —
Caytleiny	Coll. John Irwin		15 — —

An extract from a ***Rental from the O'Hara Estate 1756.*** – see page 38.

1760   Boswell Estate rentals.
Rental ledger for Ahamlish and Drumrat parishes, major tenants only. Also, an accounts book with names of suppliers, workers etc. NLI P 4937

1760   O'Hara Estate Rentals.
Rent roll for Achonry, Ballysadare, Killoran and Kilvarnet parishes, including "leases for lives" names and rent. NLI P 1923

1761-68 Rental of Charles O'Hara (the younger).
Mainly in Killoran Parish. 1761: 8 tenants, townland address and rent, NLI Ms 36,318/13; 1762-68. 38 tenants, townland address and rent. NLI Ms 36,318/14.

1768-73. Estate Papers of Owen Wynne.
List of 118 major tenants, indexed; covering townlands in the civil parishes of Ahamlish, Ballysadare, Calry, Drumcliff, Killoran, St John's, Tawnagh, Templeboy. NL MSS. 5830-1

1775–1872. Rentals and Rent Ledgers of Cooper Estate.
Rentals and rent ledgers of Cooper estate at Markree, Co. Sligo (Parish of Ballysadare). Contains rentals for 230 named properties noting tenant's name and rent only. NLI Mss. 3050-3060.

1775-1811 Rental of Sligo Estate of Charles O'Hara, the Younger.
Dated c.1775-1811. Contains approx 220 named properties noting tenant's name and rent only. All apparently in Killoran Parish. NLI: O'Hara Papers Ms. 16,712.

1783   Rental of the estate of Sir Thomas Dundas.
Rental of the estate of Sir Thomas Dundas in counties Roscommon and Sligo, 1783. Lists tenants for major properties in Tirerril (13 names); Coolavin (11); Corrin (Corran) (11); Tyreragh (Tireragh) (26). Also details of lives and relations to lessee; comments on property and on some tenants. NLI Ms. 2786.

1788-96. Rental of the estates of Henry Temple.
Rental of the estates of Henry Temple, 2nd Viscount Palmerston.
Tenant's names for 128 properties, including changes over the
years and reason (dead, emigrated etc) – also notes on tenant
circumstances – 'industrious, poor, useless' etc. NLI Ms. 1565.

1790. Voters List.
An alphabetical list of voters in Sligo town and county,
including addresses NLI MS 2169

1790s. Candidate's Election Book.
This gives 1330 names (surnames beginning A-N only) and
addresses of freeholders or electors, place of freehold, valuation
and other details, landlord or connection, and observations.
NLI Ms. 2733.

1792 and 1804. Rentals of estate of Sir Thomas Dundas.
Rentals of estate of Sir Thomas Dundas in counties of
Roscommon and Sligo. Lists tenants, land quality details for
major properties in Tirerril (19 names); Coolavin (15); Corrin
(Corran) (6); Tyreragh (Tireragh) (26). Details on individuals
in lease lives. NLI Mss. 2787 – 2788.

1795. Inhabitants of Barony of Leyney.
57 names of residents of Leyney attending a meeting to condemn
the Defenders, illicit distilling etc. Sligo Lib. LIS 013.

1795 Freeholders List.
List of 1,603 Freeholders (name, address and property
valuation) NLI Ms. 3136; see also NLI Ms. 3075. Also in
McDonagh Ms. No. 21, Sligo Co. Library.

1796 Rental of Charles O'Hara (the younger).
Names of tenants in 250 properties alphabetically listed with
rent and (rare) comments. Mainly in Killoran parish. NLI Ms
36,318/19

1796. Linen Board Premiums for Persons Growing Flax.
A list of persons paid premiums for sowing flax in a scheme
run by the Linen Board. It provides the name and parish of

residence of 1,006 Sligo persons. Widely available on websites, and in archives in book or microfiche versions, some of which are indexed. NLI (Call number: Ir.633411 I7); NAI; SOG Library. and also available on-line at www.rootsweb.ancestry.com/~irlsli/sligocountyireland.html

1798 *Persons who Suffered Loss in '98 Rebellion.*
Approximately 250 names, occupation/rank, residence, and place where loss was sustained, nature of loss and amount claimed. NLI JLB 94107. Also on CD from Eneclann as '1798 Rebellion: Claimants and Surrenders': www.archivecdbooks.ie (ISBN: 1 905118 03) and www.findmypast.ie A list of suffering loyalists containing the names of County Sligo claimants for compensation in 1798 showing payments, rejections and some comments can also be found in *'The History of Sligo Town and County'* Vol.II by T. O'Rorke (n.d.) Appendix I, page 593-599. see page 43

1798. *Tenants on Wynne Estate.*
List of 360 Tenants on Wynne Estates in Calry and Drumcliffe parishes and in Sligo Town. NLI Ms 3311.

1798-1825. *Estate Papers of Owen Wynne.*
Rental and two rent ledgers, yearly from 1798 to 1825, with all tenants; covering townlands in the civil parishes of Ahamlish, Ballysadare, Calry, Drumcliff, Killoran, St John's, Tawnagh, Templeboy. NLI MSS.3312-13

1804 *Rentals of estate of Sir Thomas Dundas.*
see 1792

1805-92 *Register of Tree Planting.*
128 names of person registering their intention to plant trees. Names and townland in which planting is intended. Mainly 1805-30. Sligo Lib. Lis 018.

1806-10 *Rent Ledger of the Cooper of Markree Estates.*
Rent Ledger of the Cooper of Markree Estates. (Parish of Ballysadare) 170 names of mainly larger land-holders and middlemen. NLI Ms. 2175.

		£	s.	d.
46 Charles Wood, Esq., Chapelfield	. . .	158	12	0
47 Thomas Martin's claim resumed	. .	122	12	0
48 Rev. Isaac Dodd, Kingsfort . . .	.	9	16	4
49 James Conelly, Collooney . .	.	20	0	0
50 Wm. Scott, Carrowdurneen . .	.	57	15	0
51 Wm. Fenton's claim resumed . .	.	7	8	4
52 Jacob Martin, Keighroe . .	.	16	8	3
53 John Scott, jun., Carrowdurneen . .	.	13	1	4
54 Thomas Scott, Ardnaglass . .	.	9	4	0
55 Francis Hill, Carrownapull . .	.	3	8	3
56 James Scott, Carrowdurneen . .	.	8	18	6
57 Robert Rutledge, Knockahullen . .	.	3	8	3
58 Henry Meredith, Tubbercurry . .	.	17	0	0
59 Patrick Moore, Corkhill . .	.	80	0	0
60 Wm. Burroughs, Carrowcashell . .	.	16	0	0
61 George Routledge, Killeens—"from the prevarication of his witnesses, and from the whole of the business, not entitled to any compensation whatever"	.	Rejected.		
62 Thomas Clarke, Ardabrone . .	.	3	16	5
63 Wm. Higgins, Carrowdurneen . .	.	5	0	0
64 Charles Ormsby, Ardnaree . .	.	77	10	4
65 Mary Dunbar, Dooneane—"has proved her claim, but we recommend security to be had that the children of her late husband be secured in the above claim, as she now lives with a noted rebel."	.	14	10	0
66 Frances Armstrong, widow, of Bochane .	.	17	13	3
67 James McKim, Grangemor . . .	.	11	11	9
68 Charles Beatty, Lugdoon . .	.	9	0	3
69 Edward Simpson, Ballisodare . .	.	14	15	9
70 Patrick Coulter, Ballinfull . .	.	10	16	1½
71 Peter Rutledge, Knockahullen	.	9	2	0
72 John Smith, Quiguboy . .	.	48	5	7½
73 Thomas Fawcet, Finnid . .	.	92	0	0
74 John Scott, Ballyholan . .	.	127	3	7½
75 Margaret Joint, Ballyglass . .	.	89	11	0

An extract showing some 1798 claimants from
'The History of Sligo Town and County' Vol.II by T. O'Rorke
- see page 42.

1808   Sligo Militia
The officers of the Sligo Militia or 22nd Battalion, in 1808. Published in *The Gentlemens and Citizens Almanack* (John Watson Stewart, Dublin 1808).

1809   Rental of Cooper Family Estate.
Rental of the estates of Joshua Cooper of Markree, Co. Sligo (Parish of Ballysadare) 1809 - 1810. NLI Ms. 3076

1810   Rental of Bishop of Killala Estate.
17 Tenants in the baronies of Tireragh, Corran, Leyny and Coolevin, Co. Sligo Tuam: Diocesan Archives; NLI microfilm (n.4217, p.3888).

1813-27 Rental accounts of J. E. Cooper of Markree Castle.
Rental accounts of J. E. Cooper of Markree Castle, Collooney (Parish of Ballysadare). Approx 190 tenants names, property and rent only. NLI Mss. 9753-9757.

1814-86. Maps of King Harman Estate.
Large folio volume of 49 maps, coloured and most showing names of tenants and some neighbouring land-owners. NLI Manuscript maps: 14 A. 3.

1823-38 Tithe Applotment Survey.
See Land Records - Chapter 6 for details.

1817   List of County Sligo freeholders.
Three handwritten alphabetical lists totalling about 1300 freeholders, stating abode, freehold value and location, landlord and registration dates (approx 1809 – 1817). NLI: Cooper of Markree Papers, NLI Ms. 9759

1818-54 Workers on Wynne Estate, Hazelwood.
Six volumes containing weekly records of labourers and wages; specifying name, wage and (in some cases) a rent paid by worker to the employer. Numbers are variable by year from 70 to 9, with some additional lists of labourers hired for special tasks. NLI Mss. 9911-9916. - see page 45

	1841	Week ends						
1	Pat Derris	1	1	1	1	1	1	6
2	Luke Derris	1	1	1	1	1	1	6
3	Pat Scanlon	1	1	1	1	1	1	6
4	Pat M. Gunn	1	-	1	1	1	1	5
5	Thos Hope	1	-	1	1	1	1	5
6	Mick Cambell	1	-	1	1	1	1	5
7	Thos Carroll	1	-	1	1	1	1	5
8	James Folly	1	1	1	1	1	1	6
9	William Boyd	1	1	1	1	1	1	6
10	Mick Frizel	1	1	1	1	1	1	6
11	Thos Hargaden	1	-	1	1	1	1	5
12	Pat Cambell	1	-	1	1	1	1	5
13	Robert Lendsey	-	-	1	1	1	1	3
14	Joe Denby	1	1	1	1	1	1	6
15	Saml Boyd	1	-	1	1	1	1	5
16	James Commons	1	-	1	1	1	1	6
17	Pat Gollagher	1	-	-	1	1	1	4
18	Phelam Hargaden	1	1	1	1	1	1	6
19	Pat Healy	1	-	1	1	1	1	5
20	James Kerr	1	-	1	1	1	1	5
21	James Scot	-	-	-	1	1	1	3
22	John Gollagher	1	-	1	1	1	1	5
23	Owen Commons	1	1	1	1	1	1	6
24	Frank Hopper	1	-	1	1	1	1	5
25	Bryan Mitchal	1	-	-	-	1	1	2
26	James Dunn	1	-	1	1	1	1	5
27	Martin Folly	1	-	1	1	1	1	5
28	Thos Carroll	1	1	1	1	1	1	6
29	William Duffy	1	-	1	1	1	1	5
30	John Murtagh	1	-	1	1	1	1	5

From one of six volumes of
Labourers on the Wynne Estate 1818-1854
- see page 44

1826   Sligo Teachers.

Lists 233 teachers, address, income, religion   and details of their school. Reports from Commissioners of the Irish Education Inquiry (Second Report 1826). Also available on CD from www.archivecdbooks.ie see below

Appendix, N° 22.—PAROCHIAL RETURNS : -   -   -   -

NAME of Townland or Place, at which the School is held.	NAME of MASTER or MISTRESS.	RELIGION of Master or Mistress.	FREE, or PAY SCHOOL.	TOTAL Annual INCOME of Master or Mistress, arising in all ways from the School.	DESCRIPTION of the SCHOOL HOUSE, and probable COST thereof.
Grange -	Owen Haren and Patrick Jeelor.	R. catholic	pay	20*l*. and 24*l*.	built with stone and lime ; thatched.
Cruckill -	Felix Connolly -	R. catholic	pay	about 20 *l*. -	built with stone and lime; thatched.
Cartron -	Andrew Harrison	R. catholic	pay	15*l*. to 18*l*.	built with stone and mortar; worth 7 guineas.
Mount Temple	Denis Magowen -	R. catholic	pay	about 13*l*. -	clay, mortar and stone; worth about 2 guineas.
Bridge-street Town.	James Begley -	R. catholic	free	20 *l*. - -	built of stone and ltme ; rented at 14 *l*. per year ; probable cost 150*l*.
Gore-street Town,	Pat Cunnigham -	R. catholic	pay	60*l*. - -	built of stone and lime ; cost about 14*l*.
Holboun-st.	Frances Swords -	R. catholic	pay	30*l*. - -	built of stone and lime ; cost about 20*l*.
Bridge-street	James Armstrong & Rosanna Armstrong	protestant R. catholic	pay –	24*l*. - -	built of stone and lime ; cost new

from
'Reports from Commissioners of the Irish Education Inquiry'
(Second Report 1826). Available from www.archivecdbooks.ie
- see above

1827-30 Rental of Estates in Sligo Town and County.

Rental of estates of Joshua Edward Cooper in Sligo town and county. Rentals of ~220 properties – tenant's name, property and rent only. NLI Ms. 2099.

1828   ***Tithe Applotment Book for Dromard Parish.***
Applotment book with 400 names, details of land-holding and amount of tithe payable. NAI M941x

1829   *Sligo Town Householders in Arrears.*
Lists 75 householders by street in Sligo town with amount in arrears to Sligo Town Commissioners. Sligo Lib. LIS 019

1829   *Householders of Union of St John, Sligo Town.*
Notice listing 90 names of parishioners requested to convene to consider a local issue. Sligo Lib. Lis 020.

1829-31. Sligo Freeholders
List of Freeholders of Sligo 1829-1832, approx. 1,000 names, and addresses. Sligo Lib. Lis 039 see sample on page 48

1829-32 Applicants to Register Freeholds.
Newspaper notices indicating intention to register a freehold. Lists name and address. Lists are in Sligo Journal for the dates: 3 July 1829 (15 names); 25 Sept 1829 (54 names); Jan 8 1830 (20 names); April 9 1830 (21 names); July 2 1830 (57 names); Jan 7 1831 (47 names); June 24 1831 (148 names); June 1 1832 (7 names). Copies of all in Sligo Lib. Lis 054.

1831-32 Names of persons convicted at Sligo Petty Sessions.
97 names, offence, penalty and other court details. Sligo Journal, Mar 23 1832; Also in Sligo Lib. Lis 022. See also www.findmypast.ie

1835.   *Protestant Residents of CofI Parish of St Johns.*
Approx 900 people listed by household in each street (including some children). Some occupations and observations. RCBL P102; copy in Sligo Lis023.

1832-37 List of Voters Registered in the Borough of Sligo.
Parl. Papers 1837, 11 (2): 205-16 (835 names, occupations, and addresses).

1834   *Cess Payers*
A list of cess payers for 1834. Sligo Lib. Lis 039.

NAME	ADDRESS	LOCATION	FREEHOLD LIST	CESSPAYER
Conway, John.	Culleens.		1829.	
Cook, John.	Tubbercurry.		1829.	
Cooke, Charles.	Carrowntubber.	Liney.	1830.	
Cooke, John.	Tubbercurry.		1829.	
Cooke, Lawrence.	Curry.	Liney.	1830.	
Cookson, Thomas.	Market Street, Sligo.		1829.	
Cooney, Daniel.	Crokaghmore.	Tireragh.	1830.	
Coristine, Bryan.	Flulogh.		1829.	
Corkeran, Thomas.	Ballinscarrow.		1829.	
Cosgrave, Daniel.	Rathlee.		1829.	
Cosgrove, Pat.	Maydoo.	Coolavin.	1830.	
Costello, Peter.	Carrowmore.	Tirerill.	1830.	
Costello, Thomas.	Gurteen.		1829.	
Costello, William.	Bunafedda.	Liney.	1829.	
Coughlan, Thomas.	Grange.	Carberry.	1830.	
Coyne, Bernard.	Caltreagh, Sligo.	Carberry.	1829.	
Craig, George.	Quignamanger.	Tireragh.	1831.	
Craig, Richard.	Knockbeg.		1829.	
Crawford, James.	Scardenmore.		1829.	
Crofton, James.	Longford House.	Tireragh.	1829.	

Extract from *Freeholders of Sligo 1829* - see page 47.

1835. Chelsea Pensioners.
A list of names of 69 out-pensioners of Chelsea Hospital (British Army Veterans) residing in Sligo who have been found fit at recent examinations. Details recorded: Name, Regiment, Pension and address (Parish or Village). NAI: OP 1835/8.

1837 Voters List.
Approximately 650 names and townland address. Published in Sligo Champion Sept 1837; also Sligo Lib. Lis 060

1840s Rental of the Caulfield Estate.
Rental of the Caulfield estate in the Parish of Kilmacteige showing tenants on 284 holdings, rent due, poor rate allowed, and observations. PRONI D. 266 (339, 346)

1839 Gaming Certificates List.
Gaming certificates were issued to persons allowing them to hunt for game in certain areas for certain periods. A printed list of 44 persons who obtained gaming certificates arranged by area is available in PRONI Ref: T. 688.

1840 Petition in Favour of the Bishop of Elphin
A petition signed by 120 inhabitants of Sligo town and neighbourhood, presented to the Right Rev. Dr. Patrick Burke, Roman Catholic Bishop of Elphin. Published in the Freeman's Journal 2nd April 1840, p.1. see extract on page 123.

1842 Householders in Sligo Town.
Borough Valuation list showing 2,200 householders by name, street address, valuation etc. Divided by Ward. 700 households in West Ward; 900 in East and 600 in North. Sligo Lib Lis 056. Also indexed by SHGC.

1843 County Sligo Voters.
63 voters in all baronies: names, residence and property. NAI OP/1843/61

1845 Rate book for Ballisodare District Electoral Division.
Lists 768 residents stating Townland, description of holding (usually 'cabin and land'); landlord, and valuation and tax details. NLI Ms 16,732.

1847   Letters and Petitions from Tenants of the O'Hara Estate.
Letters and petitions seeking relief from distress and help to emigrate. 20 letters from tenants outlining circumstances. NLI Ms. 20,376 .

1848   William Smith O'Brien Petition.
William Smith O'Brien was the 'Young Irelander' leader who was sentenced to death. A petition for clemency was signed by over 80,000 people, including many from Sligo. It lists the name and address of each signatory NAI OP16/2/098 - 16/2/100. Also available on CDROM from Eneclann at www. eneclann.ie and www.findmypast.ie

1849-64 Rentals of Estate of Myles John O'Reilly.
Tenants of 37 properties in Kilshalvy (Spurtown and Ogham townlands) with rent due and some observations. NLI O'Reilly Mss: No. 8, n.856, p.1028

1850/1852 Voters in the Barony Tirerill.
List of 392 'male persons' with valuations of £12 qualifying as voters. Gives name, place of abode, nature of qualification and other property situated in the barony. Also further 30 people (larger landholders) qualifying as eligible to vote for Knight of Sligo in 1852. NLI Ms 36,423/1 see page 51.

c.1850   Mill Books.
Undated lists of millers and details of their premises (by Barony). They also include millers in County Sligo. Published as "The Millers and Mills of Ireland' by William E. Hogg (Dublin 1997).

1852   Electors in county Sligo.
Poll Books dated July 23, 1852. for baronies of Tireragh (347 names), Carberry (Carbury) (350 names) and Liney (322 names). (Each list gives residence, property in barony, valuation, date of registration) NLI MS 3064; Poll Books for baronies of Tirerrill (360 names), Corran (227 names) and Coolavin (100 names). NLI Mss. 3073-3075

COUNTY OF SLIGO—BARONY OF TIRERILL.

List of Persons Registered within Eight Years previous to the Sixteenth Day of March next, under the Provisions of an Act passed in the Session of Parliament holden in the Second and Third years of the Reign of King WILLIAM the Fourth, Chapter 88, entitled "An Act to Amend the Representation of the People of Ireland," in respect of property situate wholly or in part within the Barony of TIRERILL, as Voters in the Election of a Knight or Knights of the Shire for the County of Sligo, (except all persons registered under the said Act in respect of any Qualification heretofore requiring the Elector to be or to have been in the actual Occupation of the Premises.)

Margin for entering Clerk of Peace's objections.	Christian Name and Surname of each Person Registered, at full length.	Place of Abode.	Nature of Qualification.	Townland or Denomination, Street, Lane, or other like place in this Barony, and Number of House (if any) where the Property is situate, or Name of the Property, and the Name of the Tenant (if any); or if the Qualification consist of a Rent-charge, then the Names of the Owners of the Property out of which such Rent is issuing, or some of them, and the Situation of the Property.	Date of Registry under 2 & 3 Wm. IV., c. 68.
1	Burrows, Alexander	Carrickcoola,	£20 Freeholder,	Drumlaheen and Carrickcoola,	25th June, 1846.
2	Brinkley G. Richard	Ardagh,	50 same,	Ardagh,	9th October, 1846.
3	Burrows, Johnston	Carrowerin,	50 same,	Carrowerin,	19th October, 1846.
4	Cage, Robert Rev.	Riverstown,	50 same,	Rent-charge in lieu of Tithes out of the Union of Kilmacolm.	19th October, 1846.
5	Cooper, Joshua Edward	Markree Castle,	50 same.	Markree,	6th April, 1843.
6	Duke, John	Clogher, Co. Roscommon,	50 same,	Mountown,	6th April, 1846.
7	Elwood, Edward Rev.	Kilmactranny Globe,	50 same,	Parish of Kilmactranny,	9th October, 1848.
8	Fleming, William	Sligo,	50 same,	Carrowkeel,	26th March, 1850.
9	Ffolliott, John	Hollybrook,	50 same,	Hollybrook,	18th October, 1843.
10	Frazer, Archbold	Lavagh, County Leitrim,	20 same,	Androsna,	21st October, 1844.
11	Fleming, James	Abbeyville,	50 same,	Trien Murtagh,	9th October, 1846.
12	Farey, Ormsby Nicholson	Ardnisbrack,	50 same,	Carowmore,	19th October, 1846.
13	Guinness, Newton William	Ardootton,	50 same,	Rent-charge in lieu of Tithes off the Parish of Ballisodare,	19th October, 1846.
14	Gethin, John	Kingsboro'	50 same,	Ballindoon,	27th March, 1846. / 26th March, 1847.

Voters in the Barony of Tireril, 1850 - see page 50.

1853   *Tenants of Sir Malby Crofton.*
Rental of 86 tenants: names, rent and land area only. Townlands in Dromard parish. NAI M938X and NAI M940X

1858   *Griffith's Primary Valuation.*
see Land Records, Chapter 6.

1862   *Rental of the estates of Edward K. Tenison.*
Covers parish of Kilmactranny; townlands of Ardline (26 tenants), Cloghmine (11), Cuilnagleragh (13), Dromore (9), Highwood (7), Kilkere (2) and Moytirra W. (12) – name and rent only. NLI Ms. 2186.

1868-72 *Rentals of O'Hara Estates.*
Mainly in Killoran Parish. Names of tenants in 503 properties, rent and (rare) comments. NLI Ms 36,318/4.

1876   *Owners of Land in Co. Sligo.*
Compiled by the Local Government Board (lists 405 owners of land of one acre and over in Sligo). Sligo Co. Library.

1881-82 *Sligo Arrests.*
Arrests under the Protection of Persons and Property Act. Includes 38 Sligo persons arrested under the above act. It provides name, county, date of arrest, date of release and crime of which suspected. NLI Ms.43,233

1884   *Tenants of Thompson Estate in Knockadoo Townland.*
29 names and holdings only. Thompson Documents NAI M7126

1901   *Census of Ireland Returns.*
The official Government Census of all households conducted on Sunday the 31st of March 1901 (see introduction to this chapter). The details given in these returns are as follows: Forename, Surname, Relationship to Head of family, Religion, Literacy, Age, Sex, Occupation, Marital Status, Birthplace, Ability to speak Irish, and Infirmities. These returns are available to view and down load in pdf file format from www. nationalarchives.ie. see pages 53 and 149.

CENSUS OF IRELAND, 1901.

(Two Examples of the mode of filling up this Table are given on the other side.)

FORM A.

No. on Form B. 6

RETURN of the MEMBERS of this FAMILY and their VISITORS, BOARDERS, SERVANTS, &c., who slept or abode in this House on the night of SUNDAY, the 31st of MARCH, 1901.

No.	Christian Name	Surname	RELATION to Head of Family	RELIGIOUS PROFESSION	EDUCATION	AGE	SEX	RANK, PROFESSION, OR OCCUPATION	MARRIAGE	WHERE BORN	IRISH LANGUAGE
1	Kitty	Boyle	Head of family	Roman Catholic	Cannot read	67	F	Farmer	Widow	Co Sligo	Irish & English
2	John	Boyle	Son	Roman Catholic	Cannot read	35	M	Fisherman	Not married	Co Sligo	Irish & English
3	Michael	Boyle	Son	Roman Catholic	Cannot read	33	M	Fisherman	Do	Co Sligo	Irish & English
4	Anne	Boyle	Daughter	Roman Catholic	Read & write	32	F	Farmer's daughter	Do	Co Sligo	Irish & English
5	Tommy	Scanlan	nephew	Roman Catholic	Read & write	16	M	Fisherman	Do	Co Sligo	Irish & English
6	Maggie	Scanlan	niece	Roman Catholic	Read & write	10	F	Scholar	Do	Co Sligo	Irish & English
7	Winifred	Scanlan	niece	Roman Catholic	Read	9	F	Scholar	Do	Co Sligo	Irish & English

I hereby certify, as required by the Act 63 Vic. cap. 6, s. 6 (1), that the foregoing Return is correct, according to the best of my knowledge and belief.

John Gregg (Signature of Enumerator.)

I believe the foregoing to be a true Return.

Kitty X Boyle
mark
(Signature of Head of Family).

Witness: John Gregg, R.I.C.

53

The *1901 census of Ireland* return for the Boyle and Scanlan Family of Inishmurray Island.

1907 *Evicted Tenants.*

Lists of persons who applied to the Estates Commissioners Office as evicted tenants seeking new holdings. The details for the 29 applicants gives name, address, estate, townland, area (a.r.p.), rent prior to eviction, circumstances of applicant, and name of present occupier. Available on CD-ROM at www. archivecdbooks.ie and on www.findmypast.ie

List of Persons who have lodged Applications with the Estates Commissioners as Evicted Tenants,

Registered No. of Application.	Applicant's Name and Address.	PARTICULARS OF FORMER			
		Estate.	Townland.	Area.	Rent prior to Eviction.
(1.)	(2.)	(3.)	(4.)	(5.)	(6.)
				A. R. P.	£ s. d.
3087	M'Nulty, Bridget, Brook-street, Ardnaree, Ballina.	Verschoyle,	Cloonislane,	25 0	17 6 0
6203	Davitt, Margaret, Ardnaree, Ballina,	O'Malley Ormsby,	Farrinderouge,	10 0 0	8 0 0
1344	King, George, Knockerow, Riverstown,	R. K. Taylor,	Drumderry,	19 1 6	13 0 0
1794	Brehany, Dominick, Currownsprawn, Riverstown.	Col. Simpson,	Brickeen,	16 0 0	7 10 0
931	Waters, Patrick, Montua, Charlestown,	Messrs. Knox,	Montua, ..	10 3 28	7 0 0
5489	M'Van, Jane, Union Hospital, Tobbercurry.	Luke Irwin,	Castlerock,	70 0 0	24 0 0
3214	Kilgallon, Frank, Templeboy, co. Sligo,	B. Cooper,	Letterinchin,	475 0 0	14 0 0
6606	Walsh, Winifred, Ballacurry,	Messrs. Knox,	Ballacurry,	7 0 26	3 5 6
6562	Dowd, William, care of Rev. M. Clarke, P.P., Dromore.	J. L. Brinkley,	Knockantan,	15 0 0	4 15 0
2140	M'Donagh, Anne, Ballymote,	A. Sim, ..	Castle Ida,	35 0 0	21 10 0
5931	Munnelly, Mary, Brook, Ardnaree, ..	A. R. Verschoyle,	Cloonislane,	11 3 0	3 15 0
789	Lavin, Thomas, Murkey, Keash P.O., co. Sligo.	W. G. Phibbs,	Murkey, ..	33 1 0	28 10 4
6457	Flynn, Michael, care of Mr. Broder, Lissenagh, Lavagh, Ballymote.	King-Harman,	Cloonsilla,	12 0 0	5 15 0
3951	Costello, Bartholomew, 3, Cooper-street, Runcorn.	P. Cullen,	Finuragh,	15 0 0	19 0 0
6860	Foster, Robert, Crossmolina,	Col. Cooper,	Cloughfin,	80 0 0	97 0 0
7870	Kilroy, Patrick, Carrowknellin, Kilglass, Ballina.	Reps. of J. Boyd,	Ballymoneen,	19 1 10	10 0 0

Evicted Tenants - see above

EXTRACT FROM CENSUS RETURN OF 1851.

Application No. 3101

Date of Receipt, 24. 2. 10   Disposed of,

Full Name of Applicant, *Patrick Scanlon* (c. 68 yrs)

Address, *Mrs. Mary O'Connor, Mullinabreena,*
Chaffpool, Co Sligo

Full Names of Father and Mother of Applicant, *Michael + Mary Scanlon*

Name of Head of Family (if other than Father)
with which Applicant resided in 1851.

Relationship and Occupation,

Residence in 1851:

County, *Sligo*

Barony, *Leyny*

Parish, *Achonry*

Townland, *Magherarove*

Street (if in a town),

Place in Record Treasury, £ 32/35.

Details from a *census search form* - see below.

1908-22 Old Age Pension Census Search Applications.

The Pension act of 1908 allowed persons of 70 years to receive an 'old-age' pension. One method of proving age was to apply for a search of the censuses of 1841, 1851 or 1861. Copies of search application forms (also called Green Forms) are held in the NAI and PRONI. Each gives: Name and address of applicant; Parents (with maiden name of mother); Head of family; Relationship and occupation; Parish; Townland/Street and date of application. There are 889 entries for Sligo and they can be searched on-line at www.ireland-genealogy.com

1911   Census of Ireland Returns.
The official Government Census conducted on 2nd of April 1911. Each household return gives the same details as the 1901 census plus: Number of years married, Numbers of births and number of children still living. The originals and microfilms of these returns are held in NAI. They are also available on-line, to view and download in pdf file format from www. nationalarchives.ie - see pages 57 and 149.

1913-23 Irish Army Medal Applications.
Applicants for medals for services during the Irish War of Independence. Details include: Name, 1916-1923 service units, districts and references. Held at Veterans Allowances Section, Department of Defence, Renmore, Co. Galway.

1914-18 Irishmen who died in the First World War.
Brief accounts of Irishmen in the British Army who lost their lives during the First World War 1914-1918, also known as the *'Great War'*. Details were compiled from private sources and press reports. These were published in 1923 by the Irish National War Memorials Commission. The 49,400 entries provide: Name; Regiment; Rank; Battalion; Place and Date of death and (usually) place of birth. Widely available in Irish libraries. Also published on CD-ROM from www.eneclann.ie, and on www.findmypast.ie.

1922   Irish Army Census.
A census of personnel of the Army of the new Irish State in November 1922. These returns provide: name, address, next of kin, date of attestation and age. Held at the Military Archives in Dublin. See www.militaryarchives.ie

1924   Irish Army Pension Applications.
Applications for Pensions, providing name and details of service. A search of these records can be made by post only, giving as much details known as possible, to: Veterans Allowances Section, Department of Defence, Renmore, Co. Galway.

CENSUS OF IRELAND, 1911.

Two Examples of the mode of filling up this Table are given on the other side.

FORM A.

No. on Form B. _____

RETURN of the MEMBERS of this FAMILY and their VISITORS, BOARDERS, SERVANTS, &c., who slept or abode in this House on the night of SUNDAY, the 2nd of APRIL, 1911.

Number	NAME AND SURNAME		RELATION to Head of Family	RELIGIOUS PROFESSION	EDUCATION	AGE (last Birthday) and SEX		RANK, PROFESSION, OR OCCUPATION	PARTICULARS AS TO MARRIAGE					WHERE BORN	IRISH LANGUAGE	If Deaf and Dumb
	Christian Name	Surname				Ages of Males	Ages of Females		Whether "Married," "Widower," "Widow," or "Single"	Completed years the present Marriage has lasted	Total Children born alive	Children still living				
1	John	Brennan	Head	Roman Catholic	Read and write	43		Labourer	Married				County Sligo		
2	Sarah	Brennan	Wife	R. C.	Read and write		43		Married	14 years	10	8	County Sligo		
3	Patrick	Brennan	Son	R. C.	Read and write	14		Labourer	Single				County Sligo		
4	Bernard	Brennan	Son	R. C.	Read and write	13		School	Single				County Sligo		
5	Francis	Brennan	Son	R. C.	Read	11		Nill	Single				County Sligo		
6	Lucy Jane	Brennan	Son	R. C.	Read and write		11	School	Single				County Sligo		
7	Mary	Brennan	Daughter	R. C.	Read and write		9	School	Single				County Sligo		
8	Sarah	Brennan	Daughter	R. C.	Read		8	School	Single				County Sligo		
9	Ann Jane	Brennan	Daughter	R. C.	Read		6	School	Single				County Sligo		
10	Kate	Brennan	Daughter	R. C.									County Sligo		
11															
12															
13															
14															
15															

I hereby certify, as required by the Act 10 Edw. VII., and 1 Geo. V., cap. 11, that the foregoing Return is correct, according to the best of my knowledge and belief.

_____ Signature of Enumerator.

I believe the foregoing to be a true Return.

John Brennan Signature of Head of Family.

The *1911 census of Ireland* return for the Brennan Family of Vernon Street (now Pilkington Terrace), Sligo.

Other Sources

In addition to the above sources, there are also records which are either undated, for a wide time period or on a particular subject. Some can provide interesting family details or links:

1593-1860. Alumni Dublinenses.

A 'Register of the Students, Graduates, Professors and Provosts of Trinity College, in the University of Dublin ..'. Gives details of dates of admission, father's name and occupation, subject and date of degrees (where relevant) etc. Compiled by G.D.Burtchaell (q.v.) and T.U. Sadlier (pub. Thom's Dublin 1935). On CD from www.archivecdbooks.ie and www.findmypast.ie - see below.

PHIBBS (PHIPPS), CHARLES, Pen. (Mr Meares), July 2, 1776 ; s. of Harloe, Generosus ; b. Co. Sligo   [*N.F.P.*] B.A. Vern. 1781.

PHIBBS, CHARLES, Pen. (Mr Lyons), July 1, 1811, aged 16 ; s. of Charles, Generosus ; b. Sligo.

PHIBBS (PHIPPS), JOHN P., Pen. (Mr Lee), Nov. 6, 1815, aged 18 ; s. of Benjamin, Juridicus ; b. Cork.   B.A. Vern 1820.

PHIBBS, OWEN, S.C. (P.T.), July 7, 1828, aged 17 ; s. of Owen, Generosus ; b. Co. Sligo.   B.A. Æst. 1832.

Typical entries from the
Alumni Dublinenses 1593-1860.

1703 - 1838. Convert Rolls

An index by surname of over 5,500 people who converted from Catholicism to Church of Ireland during the period 1703 - 1838. Edited and indexed by Eileen O'Byrne and published by the Irish Manuscripts Commission (Dublin 1981).

1814 - 1922. Royal Irish Constabulary
The first Irish police force was the Irish Peace Preservation Force of 1814. In 1836 the Irish Constabulary was formed, and was renamed the Royal Irish Constabulary in 1867. During its existence some 90,000 men enrolled. The records are held by the Public Record Office in London and a microfilm copy is available in the NAI. The records are indexed by the initial letter of the surname in two periods i.e. 1816-67 and 1867-1922. They contain the following details: Name; Age when appointed; Height; Native County; Religion; Date of marriage; Native county of wife; and Dates of appointments, allocations, transfers, promotions; rewards/marks of distinction etc., punishments etc. It also specifies when discharged, dismissed, resigned, died or pensioned.

The index and details can be consulted at the NAI (Ref. MFA 24/1-16) or Public Record Office. London (Ref. HO 184.43). RIC. Directories for the years 1840-45, 1857, 1876-79 and 1881-1921 are also available in the National Library of Ireland.

1836-1924 Prison Records
Records of Prisoners committed to Sligo Prison (1836-1924) are in the NAI and also available on www.findmypast.ie - see page 151

1854-1910 Petty Sessions (Court) Records
Petty session records of those tried for minor crimes in the 'Petty Sessions' courts are available for the court in Ballymote, Sligo (1854-1910) but also for the court in the neighbouring Ballina, Mayo (1889-). These are rich resources as they provide names of accused, injured parties and others. Original records are in the NAI and also available on www.findmypast.ie - see page 151.

1923 Thom's Irish Who's Who (First Edition)
A biographical book of reference of prominent men and women in Irish life. Includes short biographies and addresses for over 50 natives, residents and officials of Sligo. Available from www.archivecdbooks.ie

any other place heretofore made use of for publick divine worship in the said parish be never hereafter esteemed or reputed the parish church of the said parish. Witness our hands and seals this 8th day of April, 1720. And your petitioners as in duty bound will ever pray.

Tobias Caulfield,
Js. Bronton,
Thomas Rutledge, } Churchwardens.
Joshua Cooper,
Thomas Jenkins,
Ino. Palmer,
H. Loriman,
Edwd. Braxton,
John Audley,
Matt Phibbs,
Lau. Bettridge,
Thos. Sweeney,
Thomas Maxfield,
Alexander Morrison,
Edward Fletcher,
John Chapman,
Philip Vint,
Mauris Freeman,
George Thompson,
John Leacock,
William Ginks,
James Wither,
Archibald Hamilton,
James Lindsay,
John King,
John Adcox,

Petition dated 1720 from the churchwardens and parishioners of Ballysadare to have the place of worship moved to a more convenient place in Collooney - from *'History Antiquities and Present State of the Parishes of Ballysadare and Kilvarnet'* p.121-122

Chapter 5   Church Records

As the civil registration of births, marriages and deaths only began in 1864 (except non-Catholic marriages in 1845) we are dependent on the records of various churches for evidence of earlier family events. All denominations have their own parish structures, and their own practices for recording information on their parishioners. However, the records often do not exist because of the inability or laxity of the clergy, or because of the destruction of the records. The availability and quality of church records varies greatly between denominations. The reasons for this are many. The Catholic church was repressed for long periods of history and this obviously affected their capacity for record-keeping. Other records were never created due to the ineptitude or lack of resources of the clergymen, while other records were destroyed, notably in the Public Record Office fire. A full account of the history and survival of the records of all denominations is given in 'Irish Church Records' (Flyleaf Press 2001).

In Sligo, the major denominations are Roman Catholic (90% of the population in 1861) and Church of Ireland (8.4%), while the other denominations totalled 1.3% of the population in that year.

The percentage of membership of each of the major religions in the province of Connaught in the 1861 census				
	Catholic	Protestant	Presbyterian	Methodist
Galway	96.5	3.0	0.2	0.2
Leitrim	89.8	9.1	0.3	0.8
Mayo	96.8	2.6	0.4	0.2
Roscommon	96.1	3.6	0.2	0.1
SLIGO	90.1	8.4	0.7	0.6

As church parish boundaries are not always easy to identify, the researcher should always consider searching the records of a neighbouring parish when an ancestor is proving difficult to locate.

Surviving Church Records

Listed below are the surviving church records arranged by civil parish, indicating the time-frame for record availability and the repositories in which they are held.

ROMAN CATHOLIC

Each Catholic parish is an independent unit and the records created within each parish are still held in the parish, although indexes and copies will exist within the Heritage Centre (see page 154). The original records may be inspected with the permission of the parish priest, but as they have been made available for indexing and filming, most priests prefer that you access these copies rather than the originals. Roman Catholic parishes are grouped into dioceses. However, there are few useful records known to exist at diocesan level.

Sligo Catholic records are relatively sparse in comparison to many Irish counties. There are 23 parishes within the county and the earliest register starts in 1796. Of these 23, the records of 14 start after 1840. A few points to note are:

- Many churches are named after ancient locations, and may not have the same name as the Civil Parish,

- Some large civil parishes (e.g. Achonry) have several Catholic parishes contained. They are indicated eg. Achonry (1) and (2) etc

- In one instance (Kilcolman) the parish church is located in a neighbouring county.

The location of each church has been given in the list below. The list is organised by Civil Parish, and indicates the Catholic parish(es) serving the area (and its location if not the same as the parish name), the map reference, date of its records, and where they may be obtained. All registers have been indexed by SHGC (see page 154) and can be searched for a fee. The SHGC records can also be checked for updates on the Irish Roots website at www.irish-roots.ie.

These records are also available on microfilm in NLI and SLC.

Civil Parish: Achonry (1)
Map Grid: 19
RC Parish: Clonacool; (located in Tubbercurry)
also Achonry and Curry, see below
Earliest Record: b. 10.1859; m. 10.1859
Status: LC: Indexed by SHGC

Civil Parish: Achonry (2)
Map Grid: 19
RC Parish: Achonry (located in Lavagh, Ballymote)
Earliest Record: b. 1878; m. 8.1865
Status: LC: Indexed by SHGC

Civil Parish: Achonry (3)
Map Grid: 19
RC Parish: Curry (located in Ballymote)
Earliest Record: b. 10.1867; m. 11.1867
Status: LC: Indexed by SHGC

Civil Parish: Aghanagh
Map Grid: 38
RC Parish: Aghanagh (located in Ballinafad, Boyle)
Earliest Record: b. 6.1803; m. 1.1800; d. 3.1800
Missing Dates: b. 1.1808-10.1816, 1.1819-1.1821, 11.1841-1.1844; m.
6.1802-4.1829, 3.1850-11.1858; d. 3.1802-11.1822, 9.1846-11.1858,
ends 1874.
Status: LC: Indexed by SHGC (b and m only)

Civil Parish: Ahamlish
Map Grid: 1
RC Parish: Ahamlish (located in Cliffoney)
Earliest Record: b. 11.1796; m. 12.1796; d. 11.1796
Missing Dates: b. 5.1829-1.1831, 11.1835-9.1836; d. 10.1822-1.1827,
ends 7.1845
Status: LC: Indexed by SHGC (b and d only)

Civil Parish: Ballynakill
Map Grid: 31
RC Parish: Riverstown, see Kilmacallan

Civil Parish: Ballysadare
Map Grid: 16
RC Parish: Ballysodare and Kilvarnet (located in Ballisodare)
Earliest Record: b. 4.1842; m. 1.1858
Missing Dates: b. 8.1853-2.1858
Status: LC: Indexed by SHGC

Civil Parish: Ballysumaghan
Map Grid: 30
RC Parish: Riverstown or Sooey, see Kilmacallan

Civil Parish: Calry
Map Grid: 4
RC Parish: Sligo, see St. John's

Civil Parish: Castleconor
Map Grid: 14
RC Parish: Castleconor (located in Corballa, Ballina)
Earliest Record: b. 1.1835; m. 10.1835; d.1847
Status: LC: Indexed by SHGC and also available on-line at www.
rootsweb.ancestry.com/~irlsli/sligocountyireland.html

Civil Parish: Cloonoghil
Map Grid: 23
RC Parish: Kilshalvey, etc., see Kilturra, Co. Mayo

Civil Parish: Dromard
Map Grid: 13
RC Parish: see Skreen

Civil Parish: Drumcliff
Map Grid: 3
RC Parish: Drumcliff
Earliest Record: b. 5.1841; m. 1.1865
Status: LC: Indexed by SHGC

Civil Parish: Drumcolumb
Map Grid: 32
RC Parish: Riverstown, see Kilmacallan

Civil Parish: Drumrat
Map Grid: 27
RC Parish: Drumrat (located in Keash, Ballymote)
Earliest Record: b. 11.1843; m. 1833
Missing Dates: b. 3.1855-1.1874; m. 5.1851-12.1872
Status: LC: Indexed by SHGC

Civil Parish: Easky
Map Grid: 9
RC Parish: Easkey (located in Easky, Ballina, Sligo)
Earliest Record: b. 6.1864; m.1898
Status: LC: Indexed by SHGC

Civil Parish: Emlaghfad
Map Grid: 21
RC Parish: Emlefad and Kilmorgan (located in Ballymote)
Earliest Record: b. 7.1856; m. 8.1824
Status: LC: Indexed by SHGC

Civil Parish: Kilcolman
Map Grid: 40
RC Parish: Kilfree and Killaraght; also Ballaghadereen (Co. Roscommon, see www.rootsireland.com

Civil Parish: Kilfree
Map Grid: 39
RC Parish: see Killaraght

Civil Parish: Kilglass
Map Grid: 8
RC Parish: Kilglass (located in Ballyglass, Enniscrone)
Earliest Record: b. 10.1825; m. 11.1825; d. 11.1825
Missing Dates: m. 5.1867-11.1867; d. ends 6.1867
Status: LC: Indexed by SHGC

Civil Parish: Killadoon
Map Grid: 35
RC Parish: Geevagh; see Kilmactranny

Civil Parish: Killaraght (located in Gurteen)
Map Grid: 41
RC Parish: Kilfree and Killaraght
Earliest Record: b. 5.1873; m. 2.1844
Status: LC: Indexed by SHGC

Civil Parish: Killaspugbrone
Map Grid: 5
RC Parish: Sligo, see St. John's

Civil Parish: Killerry
Map Grid: 28
RC Parish: Kilfree and Killanumerry (partly Co. Leitrim)
Earliest Record: m. 1827-1899
Status: LC, Indexed by SHGC

Civil Parish: Killoran
Map Grid: 17
RC Parish: Killoran (located in Coolaney)
Earliest Record: b. 4.1878; m. 4.1846
Status: LC: Indexed by SHGC

Civil Parish: Kilmacallan
Map Grid: 34
RC Parish: Riverstown (Taunagh or Sooey)
Earliest Record: b. 11.1803; m. 11.1803 d. 1836-
Missing Dates: m. 1.1829-5.1836
Status: LC: Indexed by SHGC

Civil Parish: Kilmacowen
Map Grid: 7
RC Parish: Sligo, see St. John's

Civil Parish: Kilmacshalgan
Map Grid: 10
RC Parish: Kilmacshalgan (located in Dromore West,
see Templeboy for pre-1808 records)
Earliest Record: b. 6.1868; m. 1.1868
Church Location: Dromore West, Ballina, Co. Sligo
Status: LC: Indexed by SHGC

TABLE 5.2

Abbreviations and Terms Commonly Used in Catholic Church Records

Bapt.	*Baptised*
conj.	*"conjunxi": ie joined in marriage*
coram	*in the presence of*
cum dispens- atione in bannis	*With dispensation by Banns. (see p.126)*
Derelictus	*Abandoned i.e abandoned child*
de.	*"of" usually denoting a person as being "of " a particular place or a child as being "of " a parent*
Dau.	*daughter*
et	*and*
Filia	*daughter of (parent's name)*
Filius	*son of (parent's name)*
fil.leg.	*"Filius;/Filia legitimus/a"Legitimate son/daughter*
ignotes parentibus	*parents unknown*
Gemini	*Twins*
Illeg	*Illegitimate*
in tertio/ quattuor etc consanguineo	*Where the bride or groom were closely related, dispensation was needed to allow them to marry. The degree of relationship was stated in the dispensation, eg "tertio consanguineo" means that the couple were first cousins; "quattor consanguineo" that they were second cousins etc.*
Patrini	*A term occasionally used for Sponsors*
Peregrini	*Travellers*
Sp.	*"Sponsoribus" ie the Sponsors or Godparents*
Ss. or Sps.	*Sponsors i.e Godparents*
Sub Conditione	*A child considered to be in danger of death, or apparently dead, could be baptised by the mother or other person. This child was subsequently also baptised by the priest "sub conditione" or "on condition" that the earlier emergency administration of the baptism had not been performed correctly. This annotation suggests that the child was in poor health at birth but had survived.*
Test.	*"Testibus;" or Testator ie Witness*
Ws.	*Witness(es) (in the case of a marriage)*

A table of Latin terms used in Catholic Church Records from
'Irish Church Records'
Ed. by James G. Ryan (Flyleaf Press 2001)
This publication provides a history and description of records kept
by the Quaker, Church of Ireland, Presbyterian, Catholic, Methodist,
Jewish, Huguenot and Baptist denominations in Ireland.

Civil Parish: Kilmacteige
Map Grid: 20
RC Parish: Kilmacteige (Tourlestrane, located in Kilmacteigue, Aclare)
Earliest Record: b. 4.1845; m. 1.1848
Status: LC: Indexed by SHGC

Civil Parish: Kilmactranny
Map Grid: 37
RC Parish: Geevagh (located in Ballyfarnon, Boyle)
Earliest Record: b. 2.1851; m. 1.1851
Status: LC: Indexed by SHGC

Civil Parish: Kilmoremoy
Map Grid: 15
RC Parish: Kilmoremoy, (located in Ballina, Co. Mayo)
Earliest Record: b. 5.1823; m. 5.1823 d.4.1823
Status: LC: Indexed by Mayo North Family History Society (see www.
irish-roots.net)

Civil Parish: Kilmorgan
Map Grid: 22
RC Parish: see Emlaghfad

Civil Parish: Kilross
Map Grid: 29
RC Parish: Riverstown or Sooey, see Kilmacallan

Civil Parish: Kilshalvy
Map Grid: 26
RC Parish: see Kilturra, Co. Mayo

Civil Parish: Kilturra
Map Grid: 25
RC Parish: Kilshalvey, Kilturra and Cloonoghill (located in Ballymote)
Earliest Record: b. 1842; m. 5.1833
Missing Dates: b. 1873-1885
Status: LC; Indexed by Mayo North Family History Society (see www.
irish-roots.net)

Civil Parish: Kilvarnet
Map Grid: 18
RC Parish: see Ballysodare

Civil Parish: Rossinver
Map Grid: 2
RC Parish: see Rossinver (3), Co. Leitrim

Civil Parish: St. John's
Map Grid: 6
RC Parish: Sligo (St. Mary's, Sligo Town)
Earliest Record: b. 1831; m. 1831 d. 1831
Missing Dates: m. 5.1855-1858
Status: LC: Indexed by SHGC

Civil Parish: Shancough
Map Grid: 36
RC Parish: Geevagh, see Kilmactranny

Civil Parish: Skreen
Map Grid: 12
RC Parish: Skreen and Dromard (located in Beltra, Ballysodare)
Earliest Record: b. 1823; m. 1817 d. 1825
Missing Dates: m. 1860-1867
Status: LC: Indexed by SHGC

Civil Parish: Tawnagh
Map Grid: 33
RC Parish: Riverstown, see Kilmacallan

Civil Parish: Templeboy
Map Grid: 11
RC Parish: Templeboy and Kilmacshalgan
Earliest Record: b. 9.1815; m. 10.1815; d. 11.1815
Missing Dates: b. 1816-1826, 1839-6.1868; m. 12.1837-1875
Status: LC: Indexed by SHGC

Civil Parish: Toomour
Map Grid: 24
RC Parish: part Drumrat; part Emlaghfad - see above

CHURCH OF IRELAND

The Church of Ireland was effectively a part of government until 1858, and its records therefore had a special status as de facto State papers. However, the earliest records for the county start in 1802. Burials were recorded for most parishes augmenting the civil records of death for which registration only began in 1864. A full account of the types of records kept by the Church of Ireland is given by Raymond Rafausse in 'Irish Church Records' (Flyleaf Press, Dublin 2001). The Church of Ireland dioceses serving the county are Killala, Ardagh, Kilmore, Elphin and Achonry.

A significant number of CofI records were destroyed in the Public Record Office fire in 1922. However, copies and abstracts of the lost registers exist for many parishes. Original copies of Church of Ireland registers may be found in one of several places. (a) in the original parish where they may be accessible by prior arrangement with the local clergymen. (b) in the Representative Church Body Library (RCBL) (see page 150); or (c) in the National Archives of Ireland.

The following is a list of civil parishes in Sligo, indicating the Church of Ireland parish(es) within it, the start dates of each type of record (and end dates if records end before 1900) and status (RCBL = held in the RCB Library – see page 150). Records of parishes which closed were transferred to the RCBL, where they are accessible for research.

Parish: Achonry
Existing Records: b. 1909- m. 1845-1899. b. 1911-
Status: RCBL: Indexed by SHGC (m. 1845 – only)

Parish: Aghanagh
Existing Records: b. 1856- m. 1857- d. 1856-
Status: RCBL (b. 1856- m. 1857-): Indexed by SHGC

Parish: Ahamlish
Existing Records: b. 1882-98 m. 1847-97 d. 1887-93
Status: RCBL: Indexed by SHGC

Parish: Ballysodare (or Ballisodare)
Existing Records: b. 1875-1899 d. 1877-1899
Status: Indexed by SHGC; RCBL (b. and d. from 1886)

Parish: Ballysumaghan and Killery
Existing Records: (volume for 1828-48 destroyed by fire in church, two other volumes since rebound as one) b. 1844 - 1974 m. 1846-1956 d.1850 – 1956
Status: Indexed by SHGC; RCBL (b. 1849 - & m. from 1850 -)

Parish: Collooney
Existing Records: b. 1877; m. 1845; d. 1877
Status: RCBL

Parish: Castleconnor or Killanley
Existing Records: b. 1835; m. 1835; d. 1834 (RCBL b.m.d from 1800)
Status: LC; Indexed by SHGC

Parish: Drumard or Dromard (including Beltra)
Existing Records: b. 1895; m. 1845-1899; d. 1895
Status: LC; Indexed by SHGC

Parish: Drumcliff
Existing Records: b. 1805-1890; m. 1845-1899; d. 1805
Status: LC; Indexed by SHGC; RCBL (b. 1805- m. 1923-)
Also NAIM.5094-5103 (b.1805-90; m.1805-1834) (9 separate registers)

Parish: Easkey
Existing Records: b. 1822; m. 1822-1898; d. 1822
Status: RCBL; Indexed by SHGC

Parish: Emlaghfad (Emlafad) and Kilmorgan
Existing Records: b. 1762; m. 1762-1985; d. 1762-1893
Status: RCBL; Indexed by SHGC

Parish: Glenade
Status: Lost

Parish: Kilglass (see also Castleconnor)
Existing Records: b. 1887; m. 1845-1898; d. 1886
Status: RCBL; Indexed by SHGC

Parish: Killanley, see Castleconnor

When Baptized.	When Born.	Child's Christian Name.	Parents' Name.		Abode.	Quality, Trade, or Profession.	By whom the Ceremony was Performed.
			Christian.	Surname.			

BAPTISMS administered in the Church of *Drumcliff* in the Parish of *Drumcliff* in the Diocese of *Eephin*, in the Year 18*23*

When Baptized.	When Born.	Child's Christian Name.	Christian.	Surname.	Abode.	Quality, Trade, or Profession.	By whom the Ceremony was Performed.
18*23* 1 June No. *305*	25 May	Arthur	John + Jane	Mc Cann	Tully		John Yeats
6 april No. *306*	22 d march	Anne	William + Jane	Curry	Cooladrumin		John Yeats
13 april No. *307*	7 april	James	Sdugh + Jane	Gregg			John Yeats

Baptism entries from the *register of Drumcliff Church of Ireland*
- see page 71

Parish: Killaraght or Kilfree and Killaraght
Existing Records: b. 1878 m. 1846-
Status: RCBL; Indexed by SHGC (b. 1878-1898 only)

Parish: Killaspugbrone or Killaspicbrone (see St. John, Sligo)

Parish: Killerry
Existing Records: b. 1886; m. 1846
Status: RCBL

Parish: Killoran (Rathbarron)
Existing Records: b. 1877-1899; m. 1845; d. 1896
Status: Indexed by SHGC ; RCBL (b.1882 – m.1845 d.1896-)

Parish: Kilmacowen (see St. John, Sligo)

Parish: Kilmacshalgan
Existing Records: b. 1880; m. 1840-1899; d. 1883
Status: LC; Indexed by SHGC

Parish: Kilmacteigue or Kilmacteige
Existing Records: b. 1877; m. 1851; d. 1884-1898
Status: RCBL; Indexed by SHGC

Parish: Kilmactranny
Existing Records: b. 1817; m. 1817; d. 1817
Status: RCBL; Indexed by SHGC

Parish: Knocknarea (St Anne's)
Existing Records: b. 1842-1899; m. 1843-1898; d. 1842-1899
Status: LC; Indexed by SHGC

Parish: Lissadill or Lissadell
Existing Records: b. 1835; m. 1845
Status: RCBL;

Parish: Rathbarron, Coolaney and Killoran
Existing Records: b.1877-1899; m.1845- ; d.1896-
Status: LC; Indexed by SHGC

Parish: Rosses
Status: Lost

Parish: St. John's Union, Sligo
Existing Records: b. 1802; m. 1802; d. 1802
Status: LC; Indexed by SHGC

Parish: Skreen
Existing Records: b. 1877; m. 1846; d. 1877
Status: LC; Indexed by SHGC

Parish: Taunagh or Tawnagh (including Riverstown, Kilmacalane, Drumcollum)
Existing Records: b. 1876; m. 1845; d. 1877
Status: Indexed by SHGC; RCBL

Parish: Tobbercurry or Tubbercurry (St. George's)
Existing Records: b. 1877; m. 1846; d. 1877
Status: LC; Indexed by SHGC

Parish: Toomour-Sligo (see Emlaghfad)

METHODIST CHURCH

The earliest Methodist churches built in Sligo were at Riverstown (1790) in the civil parish of Kilmacallan, and Sligo town (1796) in connection with the Established Church.

Sligo has had only a tiny population of Methodists at any time; 5,500 were recorded in the 1861 census. An account of one Methodist community, based in the neighbouring County Fermanagh, is given in *'New Methodist Church, Kilcoo, Sligo, mainly at the expense of J. Glass of New York'*. The Irish builder, Vol. XXXIII, No. 747, p. 33, February 1, 1891. A further useful source of background information on the records and history of this church is the chapter on Methodist Records in 'Irish Church Records' (Flyleaf Press, Dublin 2001).

Methodist church records are not available for public inspection. So queries may be addressed to: Superintendent Minister, Methodist Manse, Ardaghowen, Co. Sligo. As there is a close connection between Methodist and Church of Ireland, the records of the latter should also be consulted. Following is a list of the available Methodist records. Methodist marriages are included in the civil registers from 1845.

Sligo Circuit
Existing Records: b. 1819 - 1899; m. 1846-1899
Status: LC; Indexed by SHGC

PRESBYTERIAN CHURCH

Only 6,400 Presbyterians were recorded in the 1861 census and local records are not extensive. However, Presbyterian marriages are included in the civil registers from 1845 (see Chapter 3). Burial records were rarely kept by the Presbyterian churches, but Church of Ireland burial records should be checked. Useful sources on the records and history of this church are *(a)* *'A History of the Presbyterian Church of Ireland, 1610-1982'* PHSI (Belfast 1982), and *(b)* a chapter on Presbyterian Records in *'Irish Church Records'* (Flyleaf Press, Dublin 2001).

Existing Records are:

Sligo Circuit
Existing Records: b. 1806-1899; m. 1845-1899
Status: LC; Indexed by SHGC

BAPTISMAL ROLL

Date of Birth	Childs Name	Parents	Address	Fathers Occ.
09/03/1849	Ellen Clarke	George Clarke		Shoemaker
15/08/1849	Rebecca Farrel	Frank & Beesy		Weaver
02/06/1850	Anne Cunningham	Francis & ?		Teacher
15/06/1850	Jane Colvin	Wm. & Charlotte		Farmer
14/06/1850	Eliza Lytle	Wm. & Mary		Farmer
13/06/1851	Mary Rooneen	Patrick & Biddy		Labourer
26/07/1851	Rebecca Armstrong	John & Jane		Farmer
07/02/1851	Thos. R. McConaghy	James & Jane		R.I.C. (sgt)
30/03/1851	James Farrel	Frank & Beesy		Weaver
31/08/1851	William Lytle	William & Mary		Farmer
25/10/1852	Wm. Armstrong	John & Jane		Farmer
15/05/1853	Eliz. Farrel	Frank & Beesy		Weaver
15/05/1853	Mary Rooneen	Patrick & Biddy		Labourer
18/09/1853	James.D. McConaghy	James & Jane		R.I.C. (Sgt)
01/06/1853	Robert Rupel	Robert & Jane		Scripture Reader
13/02/1854	Robert Lytle	William & Mary		Farmer
28/12/1854	Geo.J. Batten	William & Ellen		Coastguard
19/03/1854	Geo. McAlister	James & Marg.		Postman
06/11/1854	Cath. Armstrong	John & Jane		Farmer
06/04/1855	John Crawford	Robert & ?		Farmer
0?/0?/1855	John McLoughlin	Thomas & Anne		Farmer
02/02/1856	Hugh Lytle	William & Mary		Farmer
23/11/1856	Mary Jane Rupel	Robert & Jane		Scripture Reader
28/03/1857	William Shannon	Simon & Catherine		Farmer

Entries from the Presbyterian Congregation at Dromore West.
in *Irish Family History 13 (1997)*
- See below

Dromore West

Existing Records: b. 1849-1934; m. 1854-1945
Status: LC; Indexed by SHGC; see also *Presbyterian Congregation at Dromore West.* in Irish Family History 13 (1997) p. 67-91. This also contains the records of b. 1849-1948; and m 1854-1955.

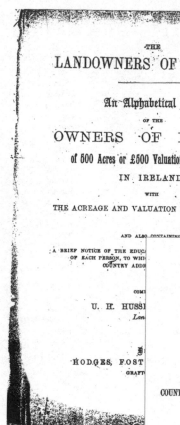

THE
LANDOWNERS OF IRELAND.

An Alphabetical List

OF THE

OWNERS OF ESTATES

of 500 Acres or £500 Valuation and upwards,

IN IRELAND,

WITH

THE ACREAGE AND VALUATION IN EACH COUNTY.

AND ALSO CONTAINING

A BRIEF NOTICE OF THE EDUC
OF EACH PERSON, TO WHI
COUNTRY ADDR

COM

U. H. HUSS

Lan

HODGES, FOST

GRAFT

LAND OWNERS IN IRELAND.

RETURN OF OWNERS OF LAND

OF

ONE ACRE AND UPWARDS,

IN THE SEVERAL

COUNTIES, COUNTIES OF CITIES, AND COUNTIES OF TOWNS

IN IRELAND,

Showing the names of such Owners arranged Alphabetically in each County; their addresses—as far as could be ascertained—the extent in Statute Acres, and the Valuation in each case; together with the number of Owners in each County of less than One Statute Acre in extent; and the total Area and Valuation of such properties; and the Grand Total of Area and Valuation for all Owners of property in each County, County of a City, or County of a Town.

TO WHICH IS ADDED

A SUMMARY FOR EACH PROVINCE AND FOR ALL IRELAND.

Presented to both Houses of Parliament by Command of Her Majesty.

GENEALOGICAL PUBLISHING CO., INC.
Baltimore　　　　　　　　*1988*

Two publications which list land and estate owners:
'The Landowners of Ireland' (500 acres and upwards)
- U.H. Hussey De Burgh, 1878
and *'Return of Owners of Land'* (1 acre and upwards) 1876.

Chapter 6   Land and Estate Records

In a predominantly agricultural community, land is the main resource and access to land is the basis of power. As in most countries, ownership of land has therefore been a major cause of conflict, both on the battlefield and in the courtroom. Transfers of land ownership and management of land rental has been a major reason for the creation of useful records for the family historian. These records can be generally classified as follows:

- **Plantations:** Land transfers to British soldiers, planters and others following various rebellions – e.g. Books of Survey and Distribution (see page 34), Cromwellian Settlements.

- **Tax records:** Records created in valuation of land for tax purposes: e.g. Griffith's Valuation; or in payment of taxes e.g. Tithe Applotments etc.

- **Regular property transfers:** Deeds etc

- **Estate Papers:** Records created by large landlords in renting and managing their properties

- **Records from other organisations**

Plantations:

Until the 16th century Ireland was very predominantly owned by Gaelic and Norman chieftains within territories which were administered by individual clans. During the 17th century this system was finally broken down by a succession of English military and legal actions which destroyed the power of the Irish Gentry. The Gaelic and Norman landowners were dispossessed and Scottish and English settlers were 'planted' in certain areas. The old and new owners of these lands are documented in the Books of Survey and Distribution (see page 34). Following the Cromwellian rebellion (1649), further land confiscations occurred and the details of this land transfer are in the 'Transplantation to Connaught' (see page 34).

Tax Records:

Griffith's Valuation.

The Primary Valuation (or Griffith's Valuation) was conducted to estimate the productive value of land as a means of establishing the level of rates (local tax) to be paid by each landholder or leaseholder. The resulting record, Griffith's Valuation, lists land- or householders in every townland and a description of the property (e.g., land; house; house and land; or house, out-offices/out buildings, and land). It also lists the landlord and the annual valuation. Because of the shortage of other records this is a very important substitute census, although note that it only lists the heads of households. It is particularly important in emigrant family research as it was carried out during a period when much emigration occurred, and thus it can form a useful link between the information available about the local origins of an emigrant ancestor and the Irish records. Microfilmed copies of the survey are available in several libraries and it is also available on-line at http://www.askaboutireland.ie/griffith-valuation/index.xml and other sites.

As noted above, Griffith's was the Primary Valuation, and the land information it provided has been maintained and updated ever since to indicate changes of ownership and land improvement, etc. As the occupiers died, moved or sold their land the records were amended to indicate the new occupiers. A colour code system was used to indicate different changes. When the record-books filled with records, new books ('Current Land Books') were used and the 'Cancelled Land Books' were archived. These can be inspected in the Valuation Office in Dublin (see page 150) and provide a history of every property holding in Ireland. It is possible to follow a chain of land occupancy from the date of the original valuation to the present. The dates of a change of occupancy can be very useful in family research as it may indicate a date of death of the previous occupier.

During the process of conducting the survey, notebooks were kept by the surveyors with information on the buildings and land they surveyed. these contain three types of data: Field Books, House Books, and

PARISH OF KILGLASS.

No. and Letters of Reference to Map.	Names. Townlands and Occupiers.	Names. Immediate Lessors.	Description of Tenement.	Area. A. R. P.	Rateable Annual Valuation. Land. £ s. d.	Rateable Annual Valuation. Buildings. £ s. d.	Total Annual Valuation of Rateable Property. £ s. d.
	CARROWCOLLER—*continued.*						
2	Gerrard Beatty,	Tobias Kirkwood,	Land and herd's house,	72 0 20	37 10 0	0 5 0	37 15 0
3	Thomas Hannon,	Same,	Land,	14 3 32	6 0 0		6 0 0
3	John Hannon,	Same,	Land,	28 2 10	6 0 0		6 0 0
4	James Clifford,	Same,	Land, house, and offices,	27 0 35	17 0 0	3 0 0	20 0 0
5	James Clifford,	Same,	Land and offices,		15 0 0	0 5 0	15 5 0
			Garden,	0 0 30	0 2 0		
6	Patrick Boland,	Same,	Land and house,	25 0 18	13 0 0	0 8 0	15 10 0
7			Land,	2 2 34	1 15 0		
8			Land,	0 3 10	0 5 0		
			Garden and house,	0 1 2	0 2 0	0 5 0	
9	John Best,	Same,	Land,	4 1 26	3 0 0		3 15 0
			Land,	1 2 39	0 8 0		
10 a	John Queenan,	Same,	Land and offices,	31 1 30	7 0 0	0 10 0	7 10 0
11 b	Patrick Queenan,	Same,	Land and offices,		7 0 0	0 5 0	7 5 0
c	Thomas Conway,	Same,	Garden, house, & offices,	0 1 10	0 2 0	0 10 0	
12	Michael M'Donnell,	Same,	Land,	23 1 31	13 3 0		13 15 0
13	Michael M'Donnell,	Same,	Land,	13 3 10	4 0 0	0 10 0	4 0 0
14 a	James Bogan,	Same,	Land, house, & offices,	51 1 20	5 10 0	0 5 0	6 0 0
b		Same,	Land and house,		2 15 0		3 0 0
c	John Jordon,	Same,	Land and house,		2 15 0	0 5 0	3 0 0
			Total,	444 0 21	215 0 0	10 5 0	225 5 0

An extract from *Griffith's Primary Valuations (1858)* showing the valuations for some occupiers in the townland of Carrowcoller in the civil parish of Kilglass. - see page 78..

Tenure Books. All are laid out in tabular form, each one specifying the name of the occupier, plus other kinds of information under the various headings. Field Books are of little interest as they refer only to land and soil productivity. House Books provide very detailed descriptions, measurements, and often sketches of the dwelling houses and also of the barns, sheds and other buildings on the holding. These details were the basis for determining the valuation of the property.

The Tenure Books define the basis on which the occupier held the property. For instance, was there a lease or were they 'tenants-at-will' who paid an annual rent but had no guarantee of continued occupancy? It may also state the date of first occupancy and the duration of the lease. These notebooks may be consulted in the National Archives (See page 149). They are arranged by county, barony, parish and townland, though they may not have survived for all parishes.

Tithe Applotment Survey

Tithes were a form of tax payable by all religious denominations for maintenance of the Church of Ireland, which was the "established" (state recognized) church until 1867. Between 1823 and 1837 a valuation was conducted to determine the tithe payable by each eligible local landholder.

Tithes were only payable on certain types of land, and the survey is therefore far from comprehensive. It does not include any urban inhabitants for instance. However, it is a valuable source. The tithe records are not uniform in appearance and in most cases will record the townland, name of the occupier, area and quality of land. - see sample on page 81.

The imposition of the tithes led to a campaign of opposition which was known as the Tithe War. It was generally non-violent, although several episodes of violence occurred throughout the country. The Tithe War ended by 1839 with introduction of an Act which transferred the majority of the payment to the landlord.

The tithe records also provide good pre-famine information for the researcher who can make comparisons with the records of the post-famine Griffith's Primary valuations of Sligo in 1858.

Tithe records were compiled independently in each parish and the records are in many archives, but particularly the NAI.

Diocese of Elphin   Parish of Thampletts

TOWNLAND.	NAMES OF OCCUPIERS.	Quantities in Detail.	Quality.	Total Quantity in Holding.	Total Quantity in Townland.	Rents paid.	Real Acreable Value.
	Cuveymore McGunigle North	4 " "	Goolah	4 " "	Value of Holding 5 " "		15
201	Patt Gunigle	1 "	Goolah	1 "			15
261	Martin Harrison 1 " "	1 " "	Goolah 1	2 "	Value of Holding 63		15
					Value of Holding 1 5		15

A typical entry from the *Tithe Applotments* for County Sligo - see page 80.

The years in which tithe applotments were carried out in each civil parish in Sligo

Civil Parish	Year(s) of Tithe	Civil Parish	Year(s) of Tithe
Achonry	1827	Emlaghfad	1833
Aghanagh	1825	Kilcolman	1832
Ahamlish	1826 1836	Kilfree	1833
Ballynakill	1824	Kilglass	1833
Ballysadare	1825	Killadoon	1834
Ballysumaghan	1824	Killaraght	1833
Calry	1824	Killaspugbrone	1824
Castleconor	1833	Killerry	1835
Cloonoghil	1828	Killoran	1825
Dromard	1828	Kilmacallan	1824
Drumcliff	n/a	Kilmacowen	1824
Drumcolumb	n/a	Kilmacshalgan	1833
Drumrat	1833	Kilmacteige	1825
Easky	1833	Kilmactranny	1833

Civil Parish	Year(s) of Tithe	Civil Parish	Year(s) of Tithe
Kilmoremoy	1833	Shancough	1835
Kilmorgan	1833	Skreen	1833
Kilross	1824 1833	St. John's	1824
Kilshalvy	1834	Tawnagh	1824
Kilturra	1833	Templeboy	1833
Kilvarnet	1825	Toomour	1834
Rossinver	1830		

Deeds:

A deed is a written agreement by one or more parties and can refer to any form of activity. The vast majority deal with property transactions e.g. lease, mortgages and conveyances, but business partnerships and marriage settlements were also registered. To be legally binding, a deed must be properly written and witnessed and, after 1708, it also had to be lodged in the Registry of Deeds. The complete set of registered Irish deeds is held in the Registry of Deeds (see p 150). As a resource for family history, they can be wonderful sources, but only for a minority. Use of deeds was variable between regions and landlords. In some areas they were common, in others hardly used at all. The parties to the deeds would generally be the wealthy, but deeds themselves can also list tenants as part of the process of describing a property. They are also useful for merchant and tradesmen families. The original deeds are written on parchment and the indexes are notoriously complex to use.

There are two sets of indexes, each of which is contained within large volumes. These indexes are as follows:

Grantors Index: (i.e. person selling the land or giving the benefit). These are bound volumes arranged by the initial letter of the surname of the grantor, within a time frame. This Index provides the following:

• 1708 - 1832: Surname and forename of grantor; Surname (only) of grantee; Volume, page and number of the transcript.

• 1833 onwards: Surname and forename of grantor; Surname and forename of grantee; Location of land (not always stated); Year of Transcript volume and number.

Land Index: As there is no grantee index, and the name of the grantor may not be known, the Land Index can be used. The Land Index is organised by barony and, within each barony, by the initial letter of the townland. If a townland of interest is identified, a reference to a deed in which it is mentioned is provided. The references in the Land Indexes are arranged as follows:

• 1708 - 1832: Townland; Names of parties involved; Volume, page and transcript number.

• 1833 onwards: Townland; Parish; Names of grantor and grantee; Year of registration; Volume, page and transcript number.

Using the information on Volume, page and transcript number, the original deed can be obtained for consultation. These originals are wonderfully variable in their content and can contain a wealth of names. Persons are named as (a) a means of identifying the parties *(e.g. John Murphy, son of Michael Murphy and brother of Jeremiah Murphy)* (b) as witnesses to the deed, (c) as neighbours in descriptions of a property... *bounded on the east by the property of James Cartan* ... etc, and (d) occasionally a description of a property will include a list of the sitting tenants.

Estate Papers:

During the 18th and 19th centuries, Ireland became predominantly owned by English landlords and by Anglo-Irish families who were granted Irish land in return for various services. These lands, or estates, were typically divided into small-holdings which were rented or leased to tenants. The private papers of the owners of these estates contain many useful records, including: Rentals – lists of tenants and associated rent ledgers detailing payments; Estate maps on which the names of the occupiers of specific holdings are marked; Lease agreements

– these generally apply only to large tenants, who may themselves have subdivided their properties into small-holdings; Letters relating to estate business, eviction or other matters but which may refer to individuals; Employee lists – estates typically employed large numbers of farm and domestic servants.

Sligo has a good collection of Estate papers and several are still in the ownership of the original families. Examples are illustrated on pages 35, 39 and 45, and many more exist in private hands.

The papers of many of these have been donated to public archives, particularly the National Library of Ireland. Sligo County Library also has a collection which is listed in 'Sligo: Sources of Local History' published (1994) by the library. Some of the useful estate records sources have been outlined in the chapter on Census Substitutes. It should be noted that estate records usually contain a huge volume of papers and letters which mention many individuals. These are rarely indexed. A major resource of information on estates is the Landed Estates Database compiled by University College Galway: http://landedestates.nuigalway.ie:8080/LandedEstates/jsp/refsource-list.jsp

The major collections of Sligo estate papers are:
Estate of Francis **Boswell**: Rentals (c.1760-1786) for properties in the civil parishes of Ahamlish, Drumrat. NLI Pos. 4937.

Estate of **Cooper** family: many volumes of rentals and rent ledgers, 1775-1872, 1809/10, for properties in the civil parishes of Achonry, Ahamlish, Ballysadare, Ballysumaghan, Drumcolumb, Drumcliff, Killery, Killaspugbrone, Kilmacallan, Kilmorgan, Kilross, Tawnagh, Templeboy. NLI Mss. 3050-3060, 3076, 9753-57

Estate of Sir Malby **Crofton**: Rental leases on properties in the civil parishes of Dromard, Templeboy 1853. NAI M938X, M940X

Estate of Sir Thomas **Dundas**: Rentals (1792, 1804) for properties in the civil parishes of Aghanagh, Drumrat, Emlaghfad, Kilcolman, Kilfree, Kilglass, Kilmacallan, Kilmacteigue, Kilmactranny, Kilmoremoy, Kilshalvey, Skreen. NLI Mss. 2787-2788.

Estate of Lord **Lorton**: lease books (1740-1900) for properties in the civil parishes of Aghanagh, Drumcolumb, Kilfree, Killaraght, Kilmacallan, Kilshalvey, Toomour. NLI MSS.3104-3105,

O'Hara Estates. The O'Haras of Annaghmore, Collooney, were one of the few Gaelic families that succeeded in retaining their estates through the successive upheavals of the 17th century. In 1876 they had 21,000 acres and the archive is very extensive – the descriptive catalogue alone – see http://www.nli.ie/pdfs/mss%20lists/066_OHara. pdf - extends to 265 pages.

Estate of Owen *Wynne*: Rentals, account books and other papers (1738 to 1825) for properties in the civil parishes of Ahamlish, Ballysadare, Calry, Drumcliff, Killoran, St John's, Tawnagh, Templeboy. NLI Mss. 3311-13, 5780-5782, 5830-1.

Other Organisations.

Congested Districts Board

This organisation was established in 1891 to provide assistance to disadvantaged areas with high populations. It did this in several ways, including redistribution of land to create sustainable holdings, and relocation of tenants from untenable land. It also promoted local industries, agriculture and fisheries. The Reports of the Congested Districts Board contain accounts of this work including some reference to persons assisted, etc. Copies are in the NLI and in other libraries. Administration records, of interest to the family history researcher, are held in the NAI, but most are in the possession of its successor, the Land Commission (see below).

Land Commission

The Land Commission was established in 1881 to arbitrate in claims of unfair rents made by tenants against their landlords. It also had the power to provide loans to tenants who wished to buy their land. It later took on the role of the Congested Districts Board. Before 1922, it had handled the transfer of 11m acres of land. The Land Commission holds a large collection of land documents at their archives section in Portlaoise; however these records are not directly accessible for research. The indexes to their holdings are available in the NLI, and from this a record number or property number can be obtained. Arrangements for access to the records related to this reference can be made with the Land Commission Records Branch, Unit 11, Clonminan Industrial Estate, Portlaoise, Co. Laois. Tel. +353 57 863 4988

Encumbered Estates Court

Under the Encumbered Estates Act of 1849 the Encumbered Estates
Court (later the Landed Estates Court) was established and empowered
to sell or transfer the estates of insolvent or 'encumbered' owners.
Documents relating to the estates auctioned by the Encumbered Estates
Court are held in the NAI, and the NLI. The O'Brien Rental Index, the
Encumbered Estates Court Index to Conveyances, the Landed Estates
Court Records of Conveyances and the Landed Estates Court Index can
be consulted to obtain references for these records. The rentals, which
document the properties for sale (including the tenants) are available
on www.findmypast.ie for the period 1850-1885.

The Land Registry

In 1892 the Land registry was established to provide a system of
compulsory registration of title of land bought under various land
purchase acts. When title is registered all the relevant details are entered
into numbered folios. The details in each folio are divided under the
following headings: (i) Property location and barony (ii) Ownership
(iii) Burdens. Maps relating to all registrations are also held by the
Land Registry. A folio can be located by a name index search (when
the registered owner is known) or a map search (when the address is
known). All title registrations for Dublin are held by the Land Registry,
Chancery Street, Dublin 7 and can be accessed by personal callers.

Seal of Sligo Corporatioon 1869

1763 **Ormsby**, Wm., Naas, co. Kildare, gent.
1784 ,, Wm., Castledargan, co. Sligo, esq.
1791 ,, William, Dublin, gent.
1805 ,, William, Dublin city, esq. [See HORNSBY.]
1662 **Ormsbye**, lieut. Thos., Comyn, co. Sligo, esq.
1802 **Ormston**, Jean (Copy)
1782 **O'Rorke**, Andrew, Creevy, co. Leitrim, gent.
1761 ,, Farrell, Carrow Crum
1790 ,, Hugh, Creevagh, co. Sligo, esq.
1783 ,, Hyacinth, Ballycurry, co. Sligo, esq.
1797 ,, Mary, Toome, co. Antrim, wid.
1809 **O'Rourke**, Fras., Carrowerin, co. Leitrim, gent.
1781 ,, Hugh, Creevagh, co. Sligo.
1794 **Orpen**, George
1740 ,, Richd., Ardtully, co. Kerry, gt.
1770 ,, Richard, Valentia, co. Kerry
1810 ,, Richard, Ardtully, co. Kerry, esq.
1768 ,, Thos., Killowen, co. Kerry, clk.
1805 **Orpin**, Fras., Douglass, Cork city, clk.
1722 ,, John, Dublin, gent.
1752 John Dublin glazier

From a page in
'Sir Arthur Vicars, Index to the Prerogative Wills of Ireland, 1536-1810'.

Chapter 7   Wills, Administrations and Marriage Licences

A will is the written instruction of a person as to the division of their assets after their death. The document in which these intentions are written is formally known as a Last Will and Testament, but usually abbreviated as a Will, and there are certain legal requirements for the will to be declared valid. The signing of the will must be witnessed, and the 'testator' (the person who makes the Will) must appoint an 'executor' (a trusted person) to carry out their instructions. After the testator has died, the will must be 'proven' by a Probate court (i.e. legally accepted as valid). If a person dies 'intestate' (without making a Will) the court decides on distribution of their property. This is called 'Administration', and also occurs when a Will is deemed to be inoperable (e.g. where it is not witnessed or the executor is also deceased). In making this decision, the court will take account of the deceased person's assets, surviving family and creditor situation, and other legal requirements. It then appoints an 'administrator', usually a relative or responsible friend, to oversee the distribution of the estate as determined by the court. The administrator enters a bond for a sum of money as a surety that the instructions of the court will be carried out. These bonds are called Administration Bonds.

Unfortunately, the major collection of Irish Wills up to 1900 was destroyed in the Public Records Office fire of 1922. Few original wills therefore exist for the period before 1890, but all survive from 1904. However, useful records can be found, as the PRO/NAI have collected many original wills since the fire, and there are other forms of testamentary record which were created in the process of proving, executing and archiving wills. In addition, researchers working on the will collection before it was destroyed also created valuable records. These additional records include:

Will Abstracts. Details from Wills have been abstracted for legal and family history purposes. The extent of detail will depend on the purpose. Will-books, compiled by Probate Courts for administrative purposes, are one example. Genealogists also abstracted details for their purposes. For instance, William Betham extracted biographical details from pre-1800 Prerogative documents (in the NAI) and also constructed sketch pedigrees from these abstracts (in the NLI).

Will Index. Although most Wills have been destroyed, the indexes to the collections survive. They provide a name, residence (sometimes just a place name) and date of death of testators. These indices may be searched online through the subscription sites www.ancestry.co.uk, www.findmypast.ie and www.origins.net. Further information is below.

Grant Books. Registers indicating grants (i.e. court approvals) of wills.

Calendars: From 1858 onward (see below for significance of this date), a short summary of every proven will or administration was compiled giving the testator, date and place of death, date of probate, address, occupation, value of the estate and to whom it was granted.

Bonds. Administrators (see above) and those receiving marriage licences were required to enter a Bond (i.e. a sum of money to guarantee that their actions would be legally transacted). These bonds also contain useful information on family members.

Finding Wills and associated documents.

Finding wills and associated records is confusing and it is useful to understand some of the background to their creation. Two basic points to note are (a) there are two different types of original wills involving separate court systems, and (b) the management of probate courts was completely changed in 1857. These will-types and courts are described below.

It is also useful to note that, although the NAI is the main repository for wills, many more are in other archives and in private collections. Wills are important legal documents which were deposited as proof of property ownership in repositories such as the Registry of Deeds, and the Land Commission. They are also included in Estate papers deposited in the NAI and the NLI, and in some local libraries. A search of the NLI Sources Database (see page 152) may be useful in finding stray wills in such collections. Eneclann have published an 'Index of Irish Wills, 1484-1858, Records at the National Archives of Ireland' on CD which includes NAI and other archival holdings (www.eneclann. ie). This information is also on www.findmypast.ie.

Timeframe	Administrative Authority	
	Types of Probate Court	
To the end of 1857	*Church of Ireland*	
	Prerogative	Consistorial
	State Authority	
From 1858 to date	**Types of Probate Court**	
	Principal	District

Wills and Administrations before 1857

Prior to 1858 probate was run by the Church of Ireland. A Diocesan (or Consistorial) court proved wills which involved property within an individual diocese, and a Prerogative Court dealt with wills involving property of more than £5 value in other dioceses. Most Prerogative wills were made by the wealthy, but even small landholders whose properties straddled the border of two dioceses may be found in the Prerogative wills. The Prerogative court was run by the Archbishop of Ireland, based in Armagh. These courts maintained few records, and seem not to have even maintained copies of all of the wills they processed. However, the wills which they held were transferred to the PRO (now NAI) in 1858 and Will-books and other references were then compiled by PRO staff. The dioceses within County Sligo are Killala and Achonry, Elphin, Ardagh, and Kilmore (both of the latter having only one parish in Sligo). Each of these dioceses had its own Consistorial court.

Wills and Administrations after 1858

Following the disestablishment of the Church of Ireland in 1857, the Prerogative and Diocesan courts were abolished and a civil court system was established. It was comprised of a Principal Registry and eleven District Registries (now expanded to fourteen districts). The Principal Registry was responsible for the proving of Wills involving property in more than one district registry. It was renamed the Probate Office in 1963. The District Registry of Ballina (which is in Co. Mayo) proved wills for Sligo.

Surviving Material of the Diocesan/Consistorial Courts of County Sligo (pre-1857)

All of the original Consistorial wills for Sligo were destroyed in 1922. However, some will-books (i.e. abstracts) survive. The original Consistorial Wills and Will books for the diocesan courts around Sligo were also destroyed. However, Consistorial indexes survive for the following years:

Diocesan Court	Surviving Records and Location
Killala and Achonry	1756 – 1831 (badly damaged) - NAI also: www.rootsweb.ancestry.com also: Index to Wills - see page 90
Ardagh	Index to Wills and Administrations (1695-1858) NAI; NLI pos.1722 also: www.findmypast.ie also: Index to Wills - see page 90
Kilmore	Fragments (1682-1858) in 'Index to Kilmore diocesan wills'. Ed. Patrick Smythe-Wood. Privately Pub. 1975 (ISBN: 0950416606)

Surviving Material of the Prerogative Court (pre-1857)

All original Prerogative Wills and Administrations were destroyed in 1922. What survives are:

Indexes: The original index (years 1536-1857) is in the NAI and is arranged alphabetically by surname, giving testator's address, occupation and year of probate. An index for 1536–1810, edited by Sir. Arthur Vicars was published as 'Index to Prerogative Wills of Ireland, 1536 – 1810' (Dublin 1897). It has been reprinted by Genealogical Publishing Company, Baltimore, and is also available on several websites including www.findmypast.ie.

Grant Books (1684-88, 1748-51, 1839) are in the NAI.

INDEX TO KILLALA AND ACHONRY WILLS

Transcribed by PATRICK SMYTHE-WOOD, M.R.C.S., L.R.C.P.

Sir William Betham's copy of the Killala and Achonry Wills Index is at the back of the volume labelled "Armagh Wills Index" which today is in the Public Record Office, Northern Ireland. By kind permission of Mr. Kenneth Darwin, the Deputy Keeper of the Records, Northern Ireland, it has been possible to publish this index. The dates covered by this index are as follows :—

Earliest date of will : 27th January, 1698.
Earliest date of probate : 2nd September, 1698.
Latest date of will : 14th April, 1837.
Latest date of probate : 5th October, 1838.

Also by kind permission of Miss Margaret Griffith, the Deputy Keeper of the Records in Ireland, it has been possible to add more to this by examination of the fragments which remain of the index to 1858 at the Public Record Office in Dublin. From this it became apparent that there were some wills with dates prior to 1837 which were not in the copy in Belfast. Three lists have therefore been drawn up from the Dublin index.

(1) A list of those wills with dates decipherable prior to 1838 but which do not appear in the Belfast copy.

(2) A list of those wills with date decipherable after 1837.

(3) A list of names not appearing in Betham's copy: or, alternatively, on more occasions than in that index; none in this list having decipherable dates.

Testator's Name		Residence	County	Date of Will	Date of Probate
Allen, Wm.	y.	Colloony	Sligo	1st April 1743	———
Allingham, Richd.	Gent.	Rockport	Sligo	5th June 1819	15th Nov. 1819
Alton, John	y.	Tubbertilly	Sligo	23rd July 1813	15th Jan. 1824
Anderson, John	y.	———	No county	15th Nov. 1731	———
Arbuthnot, Richd.	Gent.	Killala	Mayo	23rd Sept. 1777	
Armstrong, Robt.	Gent.	Carrowmabley	Sligo	17th March 1725	———
Armstrong, Thos.	Gent.	Carrowmabley	Sligo	31st Dec. 1724	———
Armstrong, John	y.	No place	No county	28th Feb. 1739	
Armstrong, Arthur	y.	Townayintruan	Sligo	19th March 1776	20th June 1776
Armstrong, Thomas	Gent.	Patch	Sligo	7th Dec. 1776	8th March 1777
Armstrong, David	Gent.	Patch	Sligo	29th June 1797	15th March 1798
Atkinson, Henry	Gent.	Ratharlish	Sligo	21st Jan. 1776	
Atkinson, Robt.	Gent.	Cabraugh	Sligo	16th March 1797	1st May 1797
Atkinson, John	Gent.	Killeens	Sligo	22nd Jan. 1801	3rd April 1801
Atkinson, Charles	Esq.	Curry	Sligo	2nd June 1831	10th Oct. 1831
Atkinson, Edward	Gent.	Ballina	Mayo	No date	9th April 1810
Bacon, Matthew	y.	Cloonagur	No county	27th Dec. 1793	21st Jan. 1795
Bacon, William	y.	Cloonageen	Sligo	3rd July 1810	19th June 1811
Bailey, William	y.	Ballymote	Sligo	18th April 1827	10th August 1827

A page from the *'Index to Killala Wills -*
Transcribed from Sir. William Betham's Copy'
by Patrick Smythe-Wood
Irish Genealogist Vol.3 No.12, September 1967, pp.506-519.

Reynolds John, 1852
    Laughlin, Creenaugh, Co. Lt., 1769
    Mary, Drumlookill, Co. Lt., 1769
    Mathias, Drimbicra, Co. Lt., 1810
    Michael (Rev.), Kiltoughart, Co. Lt., 1800
    Micheal, Cornegresse, Co. Lt., 1772
    Owen, Cavan, Co. Lt., 1771
    Owen, Rim, Co. Lt., 1789
    Patrick, Foorarugh, Co. Lt., 1787
    Patrick, Farnaugh, Co. Lt., 1796
    Patrick, Rock, Co. Lt., 1822
    Patrick, Gort, Co. Lt., 1841
    Patrick, Camaugh, Co. Lfd., 1847
    Rose, Drumlish, Co. Lfd., 1791
    Thady, Ballagh, Co. Lfd., 1761
    Thomas, Mohill, Co. Lt., 1797
    Thomas (Rev. P.P.) Aneduff, 1813
    Thomas, Creevy, Co. Lfd., 1824
Rheirdon Laurence, Cooleau, Co. Lfd., 1839
Ridley Henry, Aghehedegin, Co. Lfd., 1726
Riely Bridget, Ballymahon, 1814
    Owen, 1836
Rinn Patrick, Correash, Co. Lt., 1832
Roach Letitia, Granard, 1812
Roache Catherine, Granard, 1835
Roark Michael, Keelagh, 1818
Robertson William, Cloongeess, Co. Lfd., 1744
Robinson, James, Creeve, Co. Lfd., 1839
    John, Town of Longford, 1851
Roch Mary, Granard, Co. Lfd., 1833
Roche James, Granard, Co. Lfd., 1836
    Letitia, Granard, Co. Lfd., 1834,
    pronounced invalid in 1836
    Robert, Granard, Co. Lfd., 1824
Rochfort, Elinor, Loughill, Co. Lfd., 1763
Rock Patrick, Carrough, Co. Lfd., 1801
Rodaughan Charles, Cloone, Co. Lt., 1819
Roddy Eugene (Rev.), Granard, 1755
    Foster, Longford, 1833
    Francis, *1707
    Patrick, Millican, Co. Lt., 1817
    Paul, Longford, 1773
Rodger Lawrence, Clogeen, Co. Lfd., 1816
Rodgers Michael, Toneywarden, Co. Lfd., 1801
    Owen, Durnacross, Co. Lfd., 1837
Roe Robert, Rush hill, Co. Roscommon, 1816
Rooney Richard, Granard, 1792
    Thomas, Lisvarna, 1832
Rorke John, Tully, Caragaline, 1799
    John, Cormore, Co. Lt., 1802

Ross Alexander, Lissnabo, Co. Lfd., 1785
    Charles and James (*joint*), *copy of Charles's will with probate containing will of James to whom he was executor, Jame's will originally proved 1787*, 1797
    James, Lismabeck, Co. Lfd., 1754
    James, Killashee (*see* Charles and James), 1787
    John, Brocklaugh, Co. Lfd., 1806
    John, Corrick Ross, 1839
    Johnston, Grafantrone, Co. Lt., 1766
    Laughlin, Mohill, Co. Lt., 1724
    Margaret, Longford, 1771
    Robert, Upper Lisnaboe and Cloongish, Co. Lfd., 1841
    William, Lisnaboe, Co. Lfd., 1773
Rourke Patrick, Loghend, Co. Roscommon, 1799
Royn Patrick, Lisnamuck, Co. Lfd., *1793
Ruin Thomas, Cartrongarvo, Co. Lfd., 1837
Russel Isabella, Newtownforbes, Co. Lfd., 1743
Ryan, Lawrence, Ballycloughlin, 1828
    Mary, Cartronlebeagh, Co. Lfd., 1850
    Michael, Kiltyfad, 1848
    Patrick, Drumgola, Co. Lt., 1823

St Maurice John, Longford, 1762
Salmon James, Rincooly, Co. Lfd., 1804
Sartain Robert, Killinboy, Co. Lfd., 1798
Scally Denis (Rev., P.P.), Legan, Co. Lfd., *1832
    Denis, Fisherstown, Co. Lfd., 1840
    Patrick, Throrreen, Co. Lfd., 1838
Scanlan James, Sonn, Co. Lfd., 1789
Scanlen Charles, Longford, 1785
Scott Emma Mary Matilda, Lakefield juxta Ballinclee, Co. Lfd., 1835
    Francis, Mohill, Co. Lt., 1772
    Francis, Coolebane, 1829
    Francis, Mohill, Co. Lt., 1831
Sexton Thomas, Cartron, Co. Sligo, 1817
Shanaghy Patrick, 1742
Shandly Patrick, 1802
Shanly Connor, Crosshee, Co. Lfd., 1746
    Daniel, Aghunihurtin, Co. Lt., 1706-7
    Francis, *1819
    Patrick, Lisdrumfarna, Co. Lt., 1842

A page from the *'Index to Ardagh Wills'*
Issued as a 20 page supplement to the *Irish Ancestor,* 1971.

Will Books (transcripts of original Wills). The Will-books available are as follows:

Timeframe	Surviving Volumes
1664 – 1684	All volumes
1706 – 1708	All Volumes
1726 – 1729	All Volumes
1777	Volumes containing surnames beginning with A – L
1813	Volumes containing surnames beginning with K – Z
1834	Volumes containing surnames beginning with A – E

These Will books are in the NAI and are also indexed in the NAI testamentary card index.

The Prerogative Administration records which survive are:

Grant Books, which contain transcripts of the original Grants, for the following years: 1684 – 1688, 1748 – 1698 and 1839;

Prerogative Day books for the years 1784 – 1788; Index of Prerogative Grants of Administrations, Probate of Wills and Marriage Licences for the period 1595 – 1858. It is alphabetically arranged and gives address, occupation/condition, year and nature of grant. These are held in the NAI.

Surviving Material of the Principal Registry (post-1857)

This court was the counter-part of the Prerogative Court and deals with wills involving property in more than one District Registry. All of the wills after 1904 survive, but for earlier dates the only surviving records are (a) Calendars (see page 90 for contents). There is a single index for all Principal and District Registry grants available in the NAI and annual indices for subsequent years. (b) Will-books for some for the years indicated in the table below. These are available in the NAI; (c) Grant books for the years 1878, 1883, 1891 and 1893.

Year	Surviving Records and Location
1904 -	All original wills are in the NAI
1874	Volumes with surnames beginning G- M
1878	All Volumes

Surviving Material of the District Registry

The District Registry is the counterpart of the Consistorial Court and dealt with wills involving property within the District of Ballina, which includes Counties Sligo and Mayo. All wills since 1900 survive and are in NAI. Other records are *(a) Calendars:* (see page 90). There is a single index for all Principal and District Registry grants available in the NAI and annual indices for subsequent years. *(b) Will books:* Those available for the District Registry of Ballina are as follows:

Timeframe	Location
August 1865 to December 1899	NAI – also SLC Film 100925-0
January 1914 to August 1919	NAI – also SLC Film 100925-0
July 1923	NAI – also SLC Film 100925-0

Other miscellaneous sources of will information are:
Registry of Deeds
A sizeable number of deeds were registered in the Registry of Deeds (see page 83 and 150). Abstracts of Wills registered there during the period 1708 to 1842 have been published in three volumes as follows:

Vol. / Timeframe	Author / Publisher
Vol.1: 1708-1745	ed. P.B. Eustace, (IMC, Dublin) 1954
Vol.1: 1746-1785	ed. P.B. Eustace, (IMC, Dublin) 1956
Vol.1: 1785-1832	ed. P.B. Eustace & E. Ellis (IMC, Dublin) 1984

Land Commission
An index to the Wills held by the Land Commission is available in the NLI. See page 150.

A *'Guide to Copies and Abstracts of Irish Wills'* by the Rev. Wallace Clare (Sharman 1930) is a valuable aid to the researcher, as it provides a single alphabetical index to the following collections:
• Copies and abstracts of Irish Wills deposited in the Society of Genealogists archive
• Copies of Wills in the Prerogative Will books salvaged from the PRO fire.
• Early original Irish Wills deposited in English archives.
• Copies and abstracts of Wills published in some historical and genealogical journals, family histories etc.

This guide is arranged as follows: name, address, date of probate and a key to one of the above.

Index of Irish Wills 1484 – 1858

An *'Index of Irish Wills 1484 – 1858'* provides a comprehensive index to the surviving testamentary records in the NAI. It also includes the Inland Revenue Will Registers and Administration Registers, 1829 – 1839. It is published on CD-Rom by Eneclann at www.eneclann.ie. and www.findmypast.ie

World War I Irish Soldiers

'World War I Irish Soldiers – Their Final Testament' is an index to the Wills of 9,000 Irish Soldiers who died during the conflict of 1914 – 1918, which were deposited in the NAI. It contains the soldier's name, rank, serial number, regiment, date of death, date the Will was written, war office number, war office data, record number and name of witnesses. It is published on CD-Rom by Eneclann at www.eneclann.ie

Marriage Licences and Banns

There were several methods used by the churches to ensure that there were no impediments to a marriage. The first was 'Banns' which involved the reading of, or posting of, an announcement of the intention of a couple to marry. The banns effectively gave three weeks public notice of the impending marriage so any objections could be made. The banns were read in the parish church of both the bride and groom and the church where the marriage was to take place, if the couple were marrying elsewhere. Almost no records of banns exist.

The alternative to publishing banns was to obtain a Marriage Licence from the Ecclesiastical Courts (prior to 1858). It involved a payment as a surety to indemnify the church against any damages that may arise if there was an impediment to the marriage. These sureties were called Marriage Licence Bonds. Records include:

Indexes compiled by Sir W. Betham of wills, administrations and marriage licences of the dioceses of Waterford, Elphin, Cloyne and Kilmore c. 1660-1837. NAI, Betham Mss. NLI Mf. (n.1784, p.1784).

Indexes to marriage licence bonds for ... Elphin Diocese, 1733-1845 and Killala and Achonry Diocese, 1787-1842. NAI, Betham Mss. NLI Mf. (n.1881, p.1881).

Other published or archival material

County Sligo Wills (1705-32) NLI ms. 2164.

Index to diocesan wills, ... Elphin, 1650-1858; Killala and Achonry (fragments only); Kilmore, 1682-1857; ... NAI, Betham Mss. NLI Mf. (n.1727, p.1727).

Index to diocesan administration bonds, ... Elphin, 1726-1857; Kilmore, 1728-1857. NAI, Betham Mss. NLI Mf. (n.1731, p.1731).

Index to diocesan wills, Dioceses of Ardagh, 1695-1858, ... NAI. NLI Mf. n.1722, p.1722.

A volume of transcripts of deeds and wills relating to Co. Sligo in the period 1605-1632, with indexes of persons and places, late 19th cent. NLI Ms. 2164

Will books containing copies of wills registered in Ballina Registry, 1865-99. NAI; NLI n.1808-9, p.1808-9

Transcripts of deeds and wills recited in Chancery Inquisitions for Counties Galway, Mayo, Roscommon and Sligo, with an index for all counties. Prepared for the Record Commission in the early 19th century. NAI R.C. 5/29-31

Indexes to marriage licence bonds for Kilmore and Ardagh Diocese, 1697-1844... NAI, NLI mf. p.1882

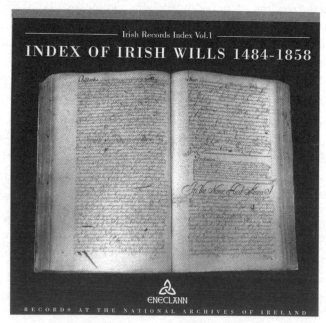

See page 97.

Chapter 8

Commercial and Social Directories

During the 18th century information on local professionals, businesses etc was made available in the form of published directories published by private companies. These contain listings of tradesmen, professionals and public officials, and some also contain lists of local gentry. They were the 'Yellow pages' of their day and different publishers had different formats for their directories. Some were national, while others specialized in certain parts of the country. Many of them contain useful information on local administration, such as the police, militia, and dates of court sessions and fairs. They are therefore a major resource for research on ancestors who were business owners or professionals, or who held some form of public office. As they were commercial ventures, the earliest directories cover the larger towns, but gradually all parts of the country, and a wide range of even small towns, are featured.

Another form of these directories is Social Directories which provide information on the 'gentry' and other prominent citizens. Some of these are contained within the above Commercial Directories, while others are separately published. Early examples include: George Taylor and A. Skinners Road Maps of Ireland (1778) and The Post Chaise Companion (1784 etc – see below). These were primarily books of road-maps for those travelling by coach through the country. However, they also list major houses (gentlemen's seats) and their owners as does Samuel Lewis's 'Irish Topographical Dictionary' (see page 18). Those with families who were traders in Sligo Town may be interested in *'Streets of Sligo'* by Fiona Gallagher (Pr.pr. 2008) a massive book which details each street in Sligo indicating name changes, traders and occupants and history.

The directories available for Sligo town and county are below. Some are available on-line from various sources e.g. www.rootsweb.ancestry or www.findmypast.ie

1784, 1786 and 1893 - The Post Chaise Companion

Provides brief details of some towns and villages of Sligo, noting local landmarks, public facilities and the seats (residences) of gentlemen and noblemen. NLI: Ir.9141 W13. The 1786 edition is available on CD-ROM from www.archivecdbooks.ie

Within seven miles of Sligo, on the L. is Nymphfield, the seat of Mr. O'Hara, near the ruins of a castle, situated on the summit of a hill. Within three miles and a half of Sligo, on the L. are the ruins of Ballysedere abbey, awfully magnificent; a mile and a half further, is Cloverhill, the seat of Mr. Chalmers; and within a mile of Sligo, is the seat of Mr. Debootes.

At Ballymote Sligo is the Hon. Thomas Fitzmaurice's extensive linen manufactory. There is here one of the largest old castles in Ireland, flanked by six towers of great strength.

On the L. of Sligo, and distant from it about a mile, is Cuming house, a very noble edifice, with beautiful and extensive parks, gardens and demesnes, the seat of Mr. Ormsby.

From the *Post-Chaise Companion 1786* - see above.

1812, 1814 and 1815 Ambrose Leet's Directory
A directory of market towns, villages and other places noting prominent residents. NLI: Ir.9141 L10. *1814* is available on www.findmypast.ie. *1815* was also published NLI: Ir.9141 L10.

1824. J. Pigot's City of Dublin and Hibernian Provincial Directory
Includes traders, nobility, gentry, and clergy lists of Ballisodare, Ballymote, Collooney, and Sligo. Also available on www.findmypast.ie.

1844 - Thom's Directories.
Annual national directory available every year from 1844, which lists public officials. Some earlier editions provide a brief historical and social background to the larger towns and villages. It is available in most libraries.

BARONY CESS COLLECTORS.

Carberry, Lower half of,   •   •   •

Carberry, Upper half of, Edward Homan, Colga, Sligo.

Coolavin, half of, Charles Costelloe, Ballaghadereen.

Corran, Lower half of, George J. Martin, Sligo.

Corran, Upper half of, Chas. Thompson, Mount Dodwell, Ballymote.

Liney, Lower half of, M. Thompson, Knockadoo, Collooney.

Liney, Upper half of, John Brett, Tubbercurry

Tireragh, Lower half of, Samuel Barrett, Cullinamore, Sligo.

Tireragh, Upper half of, G. S. Fenton, Dromore House, Dromore West.

Tireril, Lower half of, William Wilson, Bloomfield, Ballintogher.

Tireril, Upper half of, James D. Elwood, Ballinafad, Boyle.

MILITIA STAFF.

Colonel, Arthur F. Knox Gore, Belleek.

Lieutenant-Colonel, Alexander Perceval.

Majors, Charles K. O'Hara, Annaghmore, Collooney, and Sir James Crofton, bart.

Adjutant, Captain Thomas Ormsby, Sligo.

Agents, Cane & Co., Dublin.

An extract from *Thom's Directory, 1850*

1846: Slater's National Commercial Directory of Ireland
Lists nobility, clergy, traders, etc., in Ballymote, Collooney and Ballysodare, and Sligo. Available on www.findmypast.ie.

1856: Slater's Royal National Commercial Directory of Ireland
Lists nobility, gentry, clergy, traders etc., in Ballymote, Collooney and Ballysodare, and Sligo.

1870: Slater's Royal National Commercial Directory of Ireland
Lists trade, nobility, and clergy for Ballymote, Collooney and Ballysodare, and Sligo. Available on CD-ROM from www. archivecdbooks.ie

1881: Slater's Royal National Commercial Directory of Ireland
Lists of traders, clergy, nobility, and farmers in adjoining parishes of the towns of Ballymote, Collooney and Ballysodare, Enniscrone and Easkey and Sligo. Available on www.findmypast.ie.

1889: Sligo Independent Directory
Lists Ballymote, Cliffoney, Easkey, Coolaney, Drumcliff, Collooney, Carney, Dromore West, Riverstown and Bunnemadden, Rosses Point and Enniscrone, Sligo, and Tubercurry. Available on www.findmypast.ie.

1894: Slater's Royal National Directory of Ireland
Lists traders, police, teachers, farmers, and private residents in each of the towns, villages, and parishes of the county. Available on www. findmypast.ie.

1878: The Sligo Chronicle Almanac and Directory.
Complete business directory for Sligo and useful information Sligo town, and Rosses Point, Ballymote, Collooney, Ballisodare, and Easky. Also a listing of public officials and others associated with public agencies. Pub. Sligo Chronicle Newspaper 1878. Available on www. findmypast.ie.

1889: Sligo Independent Newspaper, County Directory, Almanac and Guide.

Contains a full street and business directory for Sligo borough, and a directory of the principal towns; also a full list of public officials; magistrates etc. Pub. Sligo Independent newspaper. Available on www. findmypast.ie..

CLANCY, PATRICK, Hair Dresser and Wig Maker, Castle-street.

CLANCY, CHARLES J., Agent for J Vor. Briand and Co's. Cognac and Whitham and Butterworth, London and Bordeaux, Castle-street.

COLLEARY, BERNARD, Grocer, Wine and Spirit Merchant, Knox's-street. (See advt.)

CONBOY, THOMAS, Wine and Spirit Merchant, Grocer, &c., Knox's-street. (See advt.)

CONNAUGHT WAREHOUSE COMPANY, General Drapers, Silk Mercers, Merchant Tailors, Haberdashers, Hosiers, &c., Market-street. (See advt.)

CONNOLLY, JOHN, Tea, Wine and Spirit Merchant, High-street.

CONNOLLY, THOMAS, Grocer, Wine and Spirit Merchant, Stephen-st.

CONNOLLY, Mrs. ELLEN, Provision Merchant, Knox's-street.

Business entries from the
Sligo Independent Newspaper, County Directory, Almanac and Guide. (1889)

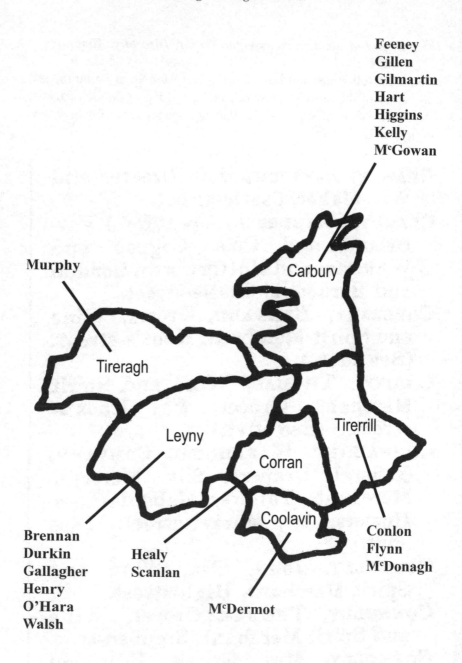

Feeney
Gillen
Gilmartin
Hart
Higgins
Kelly
McGowan

Murphy

Carbury

Tireragh

Leyny

Tirerrill

Corran

Coolavin

Brennan
Durkin
Gallagher
Henry
O'Hara
Walsh

Healy
Scanlan

Conlon
Flynn
McDonagh

McDermot

A map of the baronies in County Sligo
including the 20 most numerous surnames which occur
in *Griffith's Primary Valuation.*
see page 78.

Chapter 9   Family Names and Histories

The study of family surnames and their distribution has always been an interesting aspect of genealogical research. Whether the researcher is pursuing paternal or maternal surnames, the origins of family surnames can provide excellent directional and background information.

Surname Distribution in Griffith's Primary Valuation

To indicate the distribution of surnames in Co. Sligo a table showing the most common surnames was compiled from the surname indexes of Griffith's Valuations Survey (1858). The table below, lists the 20 most numerous surnames and indicates the barony in which they were most common at the time (see map on opposite page).

	Surname	Total Number	Barony with most occurrences (no.)
1	Brennan	261	Leyny (135)
2	Gallagher	247	Leyny (95)
3	Walsh	238	Leyny (130)
4	Hart	223	Carbury (117)
5	McDonagh	198	Tirerrill (51)
6	Healy	196	Corran (52)
7	Kelly	187	Carbury (56)
8	Scanlan	186	Corran (58)
9	McGowan	166	Carbury (103)
10	Durkin	150	Leyny (120)
11	Feeney	149	Carbury (97)
12	O'Hara	148	Leyny (80)
13	Henry	147	Leyny (102)
14	Higgins	127	Carbury (43)
15	Gillen	113	Carbury (82)
16	Flynn	109	Tirerrill (48)
17	McDermot	106	Coolavin (39)
18	Murphy	104	Tireragh (31)
19	Conlon	103	Tirerrill (42)
20	Gilmartin	100	Carbury (91)

Matheson's Special Report on Surnames in Ireland

In 1894, the secretary of the General Register Office, Robert E. Matheson, published his *'Special Report on Surnames in Ireland'*. It was based on the births registered in Ireland in 1890. Only surnames which numbered five or more birth registrations in the 1890 index were included. The figures in the following tables are extracted from Matheson's survey, showing the most common Sligo surnames as set out in the table on page 105. The first table 'Births in Ireland' shows the national number of births for these Surnames. The second 'Births in Connaught' shows the number of births for Connaught which includes Sligo.

Births in Ireland	
Murphy	1386
Kelly	1242
Walsh	932
Gallagher	488
Brennan	358
Flynn	319
Healy	291
Higgins	205
McDermot	189
McDonagh	174
McGowan	152
Henry	132
Hart	122
Conlon	107
O'Hara	105
Scanlan	97
Feeney	73
Durkin	62
Gillen	40
Gilmartin	24

Births in Connaught	
Kelly	329
Walsh	239
Gallagher	144
McDonagh	141
Murphy	110
Higgins	105
Brennan	94
McDermot	87
Flynn	85
Healy	84
Durkin	58
McGowan	54
Hart	51
Feeney	44
Conlon	42
Henry	41
O'Hara	38
Scanlan	28
Gilmartin	23
Gillen	10

Publications

The references below are all sources of family information which are either published in books or in periodicals, or are available as manuscripts in libraries. It does not claim to be a comprehensive list of such material and it is doubtful if anyone could develop a truly full list of such sources. Family histories were, and are, published by individual family members for distribution to family members. They will usually not have an ISBN number and are therefore invisible to the book-tracking processes available to libraries. Some have been presented to libraries, and are therefore publicly available. In recent years many have been made available through Google Books and other book digitisation initiatives. Nowadays a lot of such material is made available directly on websites and web-searches will usually produce some useful information.

As to the content of these sources, it is enormously variable. Some are accounts of families from those who knew them, or were them! Others are the products of research projects. The former are clearly more useful and interesting and more likely to put some of the family personality onto the bare bones of a pedigree.

Apart from the first few general references, the material is listed in alphabetical order of the family name, but note that the O' and Mc' are disregarded in this listing – e.g. O'Connor is listed under 'C'.

General References:

McTernan, John C. *'The Light of Bygone Days, Vol 1: Houses of Sligo and Associated families'*. Sligo: Avena Publications, 2010
McTernan, John C.*'The Light of Bygone Days, Volume II: Sligo Families'*. Sligo: Avena Publications, 2009.
'Pedigrees of Co. Sligo Families'. McDonagh Mss. No. 23, Sligo Co. Library.

KELLY

OF SLIGO & COLLOONEY

The Kellys of Sligo and Collooney were one of the most successful locally based mercantile families in the early to mid 19th century. With their kinsmen, the Maddens, they were to the forefront in the thriving commercial life of that era as bleachers, brewers, malters, millers and general merchants in addition to retaining their interest in sizeable hereditary leases, c. 600-acres, of fertile lands in Tireragh. They were also prominent in the affairs of the Borough as elected members of both the Corporation and the Town and Harbour Commissioners and, with the Maddens, were prime movers in the formation of the Liberal Club in 1828.

Intro to the Chapter on the Kelly family from John C. McTernan's
'The light of bygone days, Volume II: Sligo families'.

Other major sources which deal with Irish families from all counties are:

O'Hart, John *Irish Pedigrees,* Dublin 1892 - see below.

Woulfe, Rev. Patrick *Sloinnte Gaedheal is Gall: Irish Names and Surnames,* Dublin 1923

MacLysaght, Edward *Irish Families, Their Names, Arms and Origins, Irish Academic Press,* Dublin.

MacLysaght, Edward *More Irish Families,* Irish Academic Press, Dublin.

MacLysaght, Edward *The Surnames of Ireland,* Irish Academic Press, Dublin.

O'HART. (No. 1.)

Princes of Tara, and Chiefs in Sligo.

Arms : Gu. a lion passant guardant or, in base a human heart argent. *Crest* : A dexter cubit arm holding a flaming sword all ppr. *Motto :* Fortiter et fideliter.

ART EANFHEAR, who (see p. 359) is No. 81 on the "Line of Heremon," and son of the Monarch Conn of the Hundred Battles, was the ancestor of this family :

81. Art* Eanfhear (" art :" Irish, *a bear, a stone ; noble, great, generous ; hardness, cruelty.* "Ean :" Irish, *one ;* "fhear," " ar," *the man ;* Gr. "Ar," *The Man, or God of War*) : son of Conn of the Hundred Fights ; a quo *O'h-Airt,* anglicised *O'Hart.*† | This Art, who was the 112th Monarch of Ireland, had three sisters— one of whom Sarad was the wife of Conaire Mac Mogha Laine, the 111th Monarch, by whom she had three sons called the "Three Cairbres," viz.—1. Cairbre (*alias* Eoch-

* *Art* ; In Old High-German, the word "hart" (which is evidently derived from the Celtic *art*) means *inexorable.*

According to Keating's History of Ireland, the epithet *Eanfhear* applied to this Art means "The Solitary ;" because he was the *only one* of his father's sons that survived : his two brothers Conla Ruadh and Crionna, having been slain by their uncles, as above mentioned. His grief on account of that fact was so intense, that, in old writings, he is often called "Art, the Melancholy."

This Art's descendants gave Kings to Connaught, Meath, and Orgiall ; Kings or Princes to Clanaboy, Tirconnell, and Tirowen ; and with only two or three exceptions, Monarchs to Ireland, up to the Anglo-Norman Invasion. From this Art also descended the Kings of Scotland, from Fergus Mór Mac Earca, in the fifth century, down to the Stuarts : See No. 81 on "The Lineal Descent of the Royal Family of England," *ante.*

† *O'Hart* : As an illustration of the transitions which many of the ancient Irish sirnames underwent, it may be observed that, in the early ages, the "O'Hart" family was called *Cin-Airt* and *Muintir-Airt,* meaning respectively, the "kindred," and the "people, of the Monarch Art Ean Fhear" (or Art Enaar), the ancestor of the family ; but after the introduction of sirnames in Ireland, the family name was at one time *Ua-Airt,* next *Ua-'Airt* (using the aspirate before the name "Airt"), next *Ua-Hairt,* and lastly *O'h-Airt,* anglicised *O'Hairt, O'Harthiee,* etc.—(See the "Harte" pedigree, for other changes in the anglicised forms of this family name.)

Description of the O'Hart family from
John O'Hart's *'Irish Pedigrees'* - see above.

Individual Family Sources (alphabetically):
*'The **Atkinson** family from county Sligo, Ireland'* by Hanson, Helen M. Willowbrook, IL H.M. Hanson 1996
*'Pedigree of **Blair** of Ballinode, Co. Sligo c.1780 1877'.* NLI: Ms. 180, p.288
*'Another time and place: the **Black** and **McKim** families of County Sligo'*- Lex Johnson. Published by author 2009. ISBN: 9780980633313
*Papers relating to Property of **Black** family in the town of Sligo 20th c.* PRO M. 3683 (a-e)

*'John **Black** of Sligo and his Tyrone Posterity'.* Jack Johnstone. 43 (2010-11) pp 18-19.

Copies of census returns of the ***Callaghan*** family, Co. Sligo, 1851. PRO M. 5249 (4)

*'The **Callahans**, Sligo to Dakota, 1863: the descendants of Peter Callahan and his wife Margaret **Kevill** and of Cornelius Callahan and his wife Catharine **Finian**, who came from County Sligo, Ireland, to Union County, South Dakota, including all descendants through the **Baxters**, **Donnellys**, **McInerneys**, and **O'Herons'**.* Michael A. Callahan. Dallas, TX: Pr.pr. 1979. NLI GO 336

*'Historical notes on the ancient sept of **Clancy/Glancy** of Dartry'.* Maria Clancy. Dublin: Linden Pub. Services (2007) ISBN: 978-1-905487-08-0. NLI 7A1264. (Sligo/Leitrim)

*'The **O'Conor** family: families of Daniel and Matthias O'Connor of Corsallagh House, Achonry, Co. Sligo, Ireland, A.D. 1750'.* Watson B. O'Connor. Brooklyn, 1914.

*'A narrative of the important and interesting events in the history of Ireland, from the invasion of the Milesians to the surrender of Limerick. With a concise notice of the ancient **O'Connors** of Roscommon and Sligo'.* R. O'Conor. Dublin, Shaw, 1858. NLI Ir 941 o37

*'Pedigree of **Cooper** of Thurgarton and Willoughby in Co. Nottingham and of Markree, Co. Sligo 1538 -- 1837'.* NLI: Ms.171, pp.439-44

O'Rourke, Rev. T. *'History, antiquities, and present state of the parishes of Ballysadare and Kilvarnet, in the county of Sligo; with notices of the **O'Haras**, the **Coopers**, the **Percivals**, and other local families'.* Dublin 1878. J. Duffy and Sons.

*'Irish Mansions: Markree Castle, Co. Sligo. Seat of Rose **Cooper**'.* The Dublin builder, Vol. V. No. 73-4. Jan. 1, 15, 1863

'Pedigree of **Crofton** of Longford House, Co. Sligo, c.1720 -- c.1820'.
NLI: Ms.171, pp.477-8

'Pedigree of **Crofton** of Ballymurry, Cambo Castle, Mote, Lisdorne, Toomona, Clonsilla and Castle Ruby, all in Roscommon, of Templehouse, Longford House, Barts., and Mointogh, all in Co. Sligo, 1540 -- 1937'. NLI: Ms.182, pp.395-402 & 429-440

Copies of census returns relating to the Daley family of Co. Sligo, 1851. PRO M. 5249 (15)

'**Mac Dermot** of Moylurg: the story of a Connaught family'. Dermot MacDermot. Leitrim: Drumlin Publications, 1996 (ISBN: 1873437161). (SLC Lib. 929.2415 M143m)

'Pedigree of **Dillon** of Lowbaskin, Streamstown, c.1570 1682. (Sligo)' NLI: Ms.171, pp.131-3

Pedigree of **Dillon** of Streamstown (Sligo), of Stroakstown and of Moyvanmore, of Lisnegree, Killcornan, of Bordeaux, France, of High Baskin, Co. Longford, of Lungamore, Co. Mayo, of Belgart, Co. Dublin, of Brackloon, of Tolochan and of Portlick, Co. Westmeath, c.1180 1953. NLI: Ms.172, pp.52-91

Pedigrees of **McDonagh** Clan of Corran and Tirerill and Other Families of Co. Sligo. McDonagh Mss. No. 1, Sligo Co. Library.

'The **McDonagh** Family of Co. Sligo'. McDonagh Mss. No. 5 and 23, Sligo Co. Library.

'The **McDonaghs** of Carrowkeel and their changing fortunes. John McTernan'. In 'Corran Herald' No. 44 (2011-12) pp 7-8

'Pedigree of **O'Dowd** of Tireragh, c.1600 -- c.1700'. NLI: Ms.164, p.89

'A History of the Protestant **Downeys** of Cos. Sligo, Leitrim, Fermanagh and Donegal (also of the **Hawksby** family of Leitrim and Sligo)'. L. Downey. New York, 1931. (SLC Lib. 929.2415 D758d

'The **O'Dubhda** family history. Mac Hale, Conor. Enniscrone, Co. Sligo'. C. MacHale, 1990.

'**O'Dubhda**, the story of the **O'Dowda** family of kings. Mac Hale, Conor. Enniscrone, Co.Sligo'. C. Mac Hale, 1989.

Copies of census returns relating to **Dwyer** family of Dublin and to the Dwyer family of Co. Sligo, 1851. PRO M. 5249 (19-20)

*'Annals of the Clan **Egan***'. Mac Hale, *Conor. Enniscrone, Co.Sligo'*. Conor Mac Hale, 1990.

*'The **Mac Egan** Brehons'*. Mac Hale, Conor. Enniscrone, Co.Sligo: C. Mac Hale, 1989.

*'Pedigree of **French** of Galway City of Gortrassy(Sligo) and of French Park (als. Dungar), of City of Dublin, of Sunfield, Highlake and Oak Park, in Co. Roscommon, 1576 -- c.1830'*. NLI: Ms.171, pp.395-406

*'Lady Arabella **Denny** and the **Fitzmaurice** family in Ballymote. John Coleman'*. In 'Corran Herald' No. 42 (2009-10) pp 7-12.

*'Papers relating to estates in Cos. Leitrim, Roscommon and Sligo of the **French** family, with references to the families of **Ross** and **Gethin**, 1810-62'*. PRO D. 17,222-6

*'Pedigree of **O'Gara** of Coolevin, Co. Sligo, c.1580 - 1756'*. NLI: Ms.162, pp.14-15 and 148

*'The **O'Gara** Ancestry'*. By Maura O'Gara O'Riordan. In 'Corran Herald' No. 39 (2006-07) pp 32-36

*'Births, Baptisms and Deaths in the exiled **O'Gara** family'*. By Maura O'Gara O'Riordan. In 'Corran Herald' No. 42 (2009-10) pp 25-29

*'Pedigree of **Garvey** of Toolubin, Dunsandle, Co. Galway, of Ballymullany, Co. Sligo, of Tunstall in Staffordshire and of Wellington, New Zealand and Garveys of Murrisk, Co. Mayo, c.1790 -- 1948'*. NLI: Ms.177, pp.386-7

*'Pedigree of **Gethin**, Barts., of Gethin's Grot and Ballyfenatur, Co. Cork, of Percymount and Ballymoat, Co. Sligo, c.1600 -- 1907'*. NLI: Ms.114, pp.111-3

*'Pedigree of **Gethin** of Moyallow and Gethinsgrot, Barts., and of Donerail in Cork, and of Sligo, c.1610 -- c.1810'*. NLI: Ms.112, p.113

*'Pedigree of **Gore** of London of Magheraboge, Co. Donegal, and Ardtarmon and Newton Gore and Lissadell in Co. Sligo Barts. c.15501805'*. NLI: Ms.112, pp.72-3

*'The **Gore-Booths** of Lissadell / by James, Dermot'*. Dublin: Woodfield, 2004. ISBN: 0953429385 (pbk.)

*'Queries and some information on W. **Griffith**, of Ballytivnan, Co. Sligo, C. **Grogan**, of Johnstown Castle, Wexford, N. Grogan, of Cork'*. Ir. Gen. Vol. 2, No. 3, October, 1945

'Capt. Cormuck O'Hara (of Cooloney, Co. Sligo)' in 'King James' IAL' (Notes on family members pre-1700)

'Pedigree of O'Hara of Coolany and Nymphsfield, Co. Sligo, c.1580 - c.1730'. NLI: Ms.179, p.318

'Draft pedigrees of Richard Holmes of Oakfield and Clogher, Co. Sligo, with notes, c.1800 -1877'. NLI: Ms.804, p.20

'Pedigree of O'Hara of Nymphsfield, Co. Sligo, and of Anthony O'Hara, Knight of St. Walladimir and of Malta, c.1616-1789'. NLI: Ms.95, pp.20-

O'Rorke, Rev. T. *'History, antiquities, and present state of the parishes of Ballysadare and Kilvarnet, in the county of Sligo; with notices of the O'Haras, the Coopers, the Percivals, and other local families'*. Dublin 1878. J. Duffy and Sons.

NLI Catalogue of *O'Hara* papers is available at www.nli.ie/pdfs/mss%20lists/066_OHara.pdf

'Estate and family papers of the O'Hara and Peyton families, Sligo, 1701-1760. NLI MS 45,928

'Pedigree of O'Higgins of Ballinary, Co. Sligo, and of Chili, S. America, c.1700 -- 1788'. NLI: Ms.165, pp.396-9

'Draft pedigrees of the families of Hillas of Co. Sligo and Hilles of Pennsylvania, U.S.A., 1718 -- 1791'.NLI: Ms.804, p.8

Hillas family papers (40 items) are in Sligo Co. Library.

'Hillas of Co. Sligo'. Ir. Anc. 4 (1972) 26–29

'The Irwins of Roxborough, Roscommon and Streamstown, Sligo'. Ir.Gen. 1 (2) (1937) p.51–56, - see page 113.

'Notes on the Norman-Walsh family of Walsh in Ireland, France and Austria. With an Appendix on the Irwins and Irvines of Sligo, Roscommon and Fermanagh'. JRSAI Ser. 7, Vol. XV, pp. 32-44, 1945

'Pedigree of Jones of Benada, and Idryell, Co. Sligo, 1635 -- 1845'. NLI: Ms.175, pp.375-8

'Draft pedigrees of Jones of Ardnaree and Jones of Ardnaglass, both in Co. Sligo, c.1650 - c.1680 -1908, with copies of original wills and deeds, 1661 -- 1780'. NLI: Ms.808, p.6

'The Saga of the Killoran Clan'. Ann Killoran. Pr.pr. Tubbercurry 1990.

THE IRWINS OF ROXBOROUGH, CO. ROSCOMMON, AND STREAMSTOWN, CO. SLIGO.

BY
EDWARD STEWART GRAY.

The foregoing genealogy has been compiled mainly from a MS. account of this family, written apparently about 1790, and supplemented from various documentary and other sources. Regarding this pedigree, therefore, any additions or corrections would be gratefully received, and could be printed at a later date, thus rendering the account of these Irwins as complete and accurate as possible.

According to the MS. genealogy mentioned above, HENRY IRWIN, the ancestor of this family, was an Officer in the Irish Army of King William III, who, for his services at the Boyne (July 1st, 1690) and at Aughrim (July 12th, 1691) was rewarded by that monarch with grants of lands including those of Ballonaghan (thereafter called Harristown, or "Harry's town") in Co. Sligo. Certain it is that the name of Henry Irwin appears in the lists, both of grantees and of purchasers, of the estates forfeited in Ireland under the Williamite confiscations, while since that date the lands of Ballonaghan (in the parish of Kilshalvy, and barony of Corran) have gone by the alternative name of Harristown. Henry Irwin, in his will, dated September 5th, 1709, and proved July 22nd, 1718, styles himself "of Ballenaghan, in the Co. of Sligo," and mentions his kinsmen, Roger Jones, William Phibbs, and Mathew Phibbs.

The MS. pedigree, which mentions five of Henry Irwin's sons, does not, except for the statement that Erasmus Irwin, the fifth son, was by the second wife, *née* Mathews, tell us by which marriage were Henry's four eldest sons, who are here named in the following order: John, Arthur, Henry and Thomas. Further light on this point is, however, shed by the Burke Collection of Pedigrees compiled from Irish Prerogative Wills (Vol. XXIV, p. 394), according to which Henry Irwin of Ballonaghan had by his first wife two daughters (Christian and Catharine), and by his second wife the following issue : —

1. JOHN, of whom hereafter.

2. Henry, who was of Streamstown, Co. Sligo, and High Sheriff of that county in 1722

3. Arthur, who, according to the MS. genealogy was an Officer in the Royal Irish Dragoons. His wife is stated to have been Jane, daughter of — O'Conor, by Lady Jane his wife, daughter of the Duke of Gordon. We may here point out that, from the comparison of dates, Arthur Irwin's wife is more likely to have been a niece, than a grand-daughter, of the 1st Duke of Gordon, and that although as far as we know no O'Conor—Gordon marriage is mentioned in the hitherto published Gordon genealogies, the above tradition bears a close resemblance to the following facts, on which it was very likely founded: Sir Miles Crouly, an Irish knight also known as the Comte de Crolly, was, on November the 7th, 1694, given permission by the King (William III), to be naturalised in France, while on August the 24th, 1695, a similar permission was granted to his wife, Lady Ann Crouly, sister to George, 1st Duke of Gordon, and daughter of Lewis, 3rd Marquess of Huntly. It is thus more than probable that Arthur Irwin's wife was the daughter of Sir Miles and Lady Ann Crouly, and niece of the 1st Duke of Gordon. Arthur Irwin had the following issue.

(1) Jones, of Streamstown, Co. Sligo (High Sheriff 1751), who is stated to have been born at the house of his father's first cousin (Roger?) Jones of Stonepark,

'*Another time and place: the* **Black** *and* **McKim** *families of County Sligo'*. Lex Johnson. (2009) ISBN: 9780980633313

'*Draft pedigrees of* **Layng** *of Coola, Co. Sligo, c. 1700-1750 and* **Lang** *of Carneen, Co. Down, c.1700 - c. 1850 and* Lang *of Dublin, 1750 - 1780 and* **Laynge** *of Clones, Monaghan, c.1700-1800'*. NLI: Ms.811(15)

'*Pedigree of* **Leech** *of Passerk, Rathroan, Co. Mayo, of Runroe and Lodge and Hermitage, Co. Sligo, of Ballycloughduff, Co. Westmeath, c.1640--1865'*. NLI: Ms.179, pp.164-8

'*Four Irish pedigrees,* **Lennon**, *of Cloncullen, Co. Westmeath;* **Nicholson**, *of Brickeen and Ballynegargen, Co. Sligo;* **Peyton**, *of Corregard House, Co. Roscommon;* **Phibbs**, *of Leitrim'*. Ir. Gen. Vol. 2, No. 2, October, 1944

'*Chronology of the family of* **Lyons** *of Rathellen and Baymond, Co. Sligo and of Kilkenny, 1837--1900'*. NLI: Ms.812(37)

'*Business papers of family of* **Martin** *of Sligo, merchants mid-19th c.'* NLI Ms. 10,706

Census returns relating to family of Martin of Co. Galway and Co. Sligo, 1851. PRO M. 5249 (49-50)

'*Pedigree of* **Martyn** *of Tulleyra, Co. Galway, of Doebeg, Co. Sligo and of Austria, c.1690 -- 1805'*. NLI: Ms.164, pp.213-6

'*Time and Place: The* **Merediths** *of County Sligo'*. Lex Johnson Pr.pr. (2009) ISBN: 9780980633306

'*A History of the* **Milmo** *family of Ballysadare, Co. Sligo'*. Fiona Gallagher. Sligo Heritage and Genealogy Centre, 1990.

'*Draft pedigree of* **Naper** *of Tobercory, Co. Sligo, and extract of will of James Naper of Tobercory, 1786'*. NLI Ms.820(5)

'*Irish Pedigrees:* **Nicholson**, *of Ballynegargen'*. Ir. Gen. 2(2) 50 (Sligo)

'*Col.* **Oliver** *(of Sligo) in 'King James' IAL'* (Notes on family members pre-1734)

'*Pedigree of* **Orme** *of Hanse Hall, Co. Staffordshire, of Carne and Abbeytown and Fairfield and Glenmore, of Fallgarriff, Millbrook, of Belleville and Owenmore and of Ballintobber all in Co. Mayo, of Enniscrone in Co. Sligo and of Jones county in America, c.1590-1844'*. NLI: Ms.175, pp.179-87

'Pedigree of **Ormsby** of Sligo, and of Willowbrook, Co. Sligo, c.1600 -1803'. NLI: Ms. 168, pp. 342-3

'Pedigree of **Ormsby** of Louth, Co. Lincoln, of Lissgallon and Ballymurray, Co. Roscommon, of Ballinamore, Carondangan and Milford and Knockmore in Co. Sligo, and of Toronto, Canada, c. 1500 -1871'. NLI: Ms.182, pp.92-4

'Papers of the **Ormsby** family of Ballinamore, Co. Mayo, including leases, wills, conveyances, maps etc. relating to landed property, mainly in Counties Leitrim, Mayo, Roscommon] and Sligo; also, correspondence, newspaper cuttings, etc., 1636-1934'. NLI POS 8502-8503. (Mayo)

Pedigree of the **Parke** family of Co. Sligo from 1627. Dublin: Trinity College Library, Ms. 3901 (S. 7)

O'Rorke, Rev. T. 'History, antiquities, and present state of the parishes of Ballysadare and Kilvarnet, in the county of Sligo; with notices of the **O'Haras**, the **Coopers**, the **Percivals**, and other local families'. Dublin 1878. J. Duffy and Sons.

Peyton See O'Hara

'Irish Pedigrees: **Phibbs**, of Spotfield'. Ir. Gen. 2(2) 50. (Sligo)

'Pedigree of the **Phipps**, **Ffibbs**, or **Phibbs** family since their settlement in Ireland. Wright, William Ball, fl.1845-1909'. Sligo: Alexander Gillmor, 1890.

'Pedigree of **Plunkett** of Dunshagly in Co. Dublin, of Markree, Co. Sligo, and Kilsmod in Co. Roscommon, and of Warsaw in Poland, c.1550-1774'. NLI: Ms.165, pp.240-2

'Bleak House: The **Pollexfen** Ancestry of the **Yeats** Family'. Irish Arts Review Yearbook, Vol. 17, (2001), pp. 44-47

O'Reillys–Forgotten Landlords. John McDonagh. 'Corran Herald' No. 44 (2011-12) pp 4-6

Copies of census returns relating to the Savage family of Co. Sligo, 1851. PRO M. 5249 (68)

'Pedigree of **Savage**, later **Nugent**, of Little Ards and of Portaferry House and of Barr Hall all in Co. Down, of Knockadoo, Co. Sligo and Ballymadun, Co. Dublin, c.1550-c.1840'. NLI: Ms.174, pp.180-90

*'The annals of the **Smith** family of Sligo'*. Smith, Barry. Winchester: the author, 2006.

*'Pedigree of **Taaffe** of Ballybraggan, Co. Louth, and Ballynaglough, Co. Sligo, and Grayfield, Co. Mayo, and of France, 1441-1772'*. NLI: Ms.165, pp.208-11

*'Pedigree of **Taaffe** of Ballymote, Smermore, Baron Ballymote, Viscount Taaffe and Earl of Carlingford, Count of Holy Roman Empire, of Peppardstown, Co. Louth, of Corballis, of Aclere, Co. Louth, of Dowanstown, Co. Meath, c.1250 1871'*. NLI: Ms.171, pp.323-36

Copies of census returns relating to the Towey family of Co. Sligo, 1851. PRO M. 5249 (74)

*'Pedigree of **Verschoyle** of Donore, Co. Dublin, of City of Dublin, of Kilberry, Co. Kildare and Mountown, Co. Meath, of Roundwood, Queens Co. and Springfield, Herefordshire, of Stillorgan Park, Co. Dublin and Tanrago, Co. Sligo, c.1690-1891'*. NLI: Ms.180, pp.301-9

*Pedigree of **Walsh**, of Strandsborough, Primrose Grange and Millbrooke in Co. Sligo and Tullin-william, Co. Leitrim, 1692 -1939.* NLI: Ms.169, p.449

*'Notes on the Norman-Walsh family of **Walsh** in Ireland, France and Austria. With an Appendix on the Irwins and Irvines of Sligo, Roscommon and Fermanagh'*. JRSAI Ser. 7, Vol. XV, pp. 32-44, 1945

*'Pedigree of **Wood** of Lacken, Caranduff and Oldrock, and Leckfield and Woodville and Cleveragh all in Co. Sligo and later Wood Martin, 1602-1883'*. NLI: Ms. 180, pp. 252-7

*'The family of **Wood**, Co. Sligo'*. Ir. Gen. 3 (8) (1963) 300–09; 3 (9) (1964) 364–65.

*'The **Wynnes** of Sligo and Leitrim'*. Winston G. Jones. Manorhamilton: Drumlin Pubs, 1994 (ISBN: 1873437072). (SLC Lib. 929.2415 W992g)

*'Pedigree of **Wynne** of Lurganboy, Co. Leitrim, of Hazelwood, Co. Sligo and Foxford, Co. Mayo c. 1620-1888'*. NLI: Ms. 180, pp. 282-90

*'Papers of the **Wynne** family of Hazelwood, Co. Sligo,[17th-19th century]'*. Are in the PRONI papers. NLI POS 9265-9267.

*'The **Yeates** family and the Pollexfens of Sligo'*. *William M. Murphy.* Dublin: Dolmen Press, 1971. 929.2415 A1 no. 2

Chapter 10   Newspapers

Newspapers are a useful but unpredictable source of information. As today, individuals are only mentioned in newspapers for certain reasons. The major types of 'mention' that may be hoped for are:

Biographical information: Births, Marriages and Deaths are listed in some papers but (until the 20th century) these were generally only of the more prominent families.

Crimes and Accidents: Criminal trials and tragic accidents are well reported in most areas and these can produce useful details, often of an unwanted nature.

Petitions, Voters list etc. During various periods of political agitation, some papers published lists of local people petitioning for local or national causes. Some also publish lists of those entitled to vote.

Advertisments: Ancestors who were tradesmen or professionals may also advertise in newspapers. These tend to be colourful as family history memorabilia but generally do not provide much additional information other than perhaps an address.

Newspapers are commercial ventures and publishers are therefore more likely to survive in areas where the population will buy their papers and provide advertising revenue. A significant number of newspapers only traded for a few years and then went out of business.

An important point to note is that newspapers (as now) were often politically aligned. During the 19th century, they often divided on the basis of republican and unionist. You are more likely to find biographical notices in the newspaper which served the community to which your ancestor belonged. There are two main guides to Irish newspapers:

The **Waterloo Directory of Irish Newspapers and Periodicals**, 1800-1900. (Ed. John S. North, 1986) provides an alphabetical listing and description of almanacs, postal directories and newspapers. Copies are widely available in libraries or from the publisher www.nwap.on.ca/irish.html. - see page 119.

The **NEWSPLAN Project** is a co-operative preservation project for newspapers in Ireland and the United Kingdom. Their Report is available in database form on the National Library of Ireland website – www.nli.ie. The report was not intended to act a bibliographic resource, but it has come to be widely used. It arranges the titles alphabetically and by county, indicating the location of each title. It is available in most Irish and UK libraries, and many elsewhere.

The major locations for copies of Irish newspapers are the National Library of Ireland, and the British Library in Colindale in London. The index to the NLI collection is at www.nli.ie/en/newspapers-publishing-in-ireland.aspx and the British Library collection at www.bl.uk/collections/newspapers.html. Unusually there are no indexes of Sligo papers, nor are any of the Sligo papers available on digital sites at the time of publication of this book. However, this is likely to change. It may therefore be worth checking web sources such as Irish Newspaper Archive (www.irishnewsarchive.com) for current holdings. In addition, many archives are undertaking digitisation of their holdings and Sligo papers may become available on-line as a result.

The National Library of Ireland have some of their Sligo titles on microfilm and available for sale. These include:
Sligo Champion (1926 – 1929)
Sligo Journal (Mar. Dec. 1823)
Sligo Independent (1907 – 1915, 1927 – 1961)

Although The Sligo Journal was published as early as 1807, there are no copies of it before 1822. Note, however, that earlier Mayo, Donegal, Fermanagh, and other county papers may also be consulted for early notices of relevance to this county. The major Sligo-published newspapers are those listed below. The list shows, for each, the dates of publication, and the location and nature of current holdings.

3305

Sligo guardian or western advertiser. 1^1-2^{71},
26 Jan 1849-31 May 1850. Sligo. *Prpitr:*
John E. Thacker. *Pub:* John E. Thacker.
Printer. John E. Thacker. 64cm. 5d (1849).
Freq: weekly *Subjects:* newspapers;
newspapers, conservative; advertising;
newspapers, weekly: poetry: literature. *Depts:*
spirit of the press, local & national &
international news, poetry, literature,
gleanings, farmers' column, meteorology.
Colour. conservative. *Cmnts:* First editorial
states that the paper 'shall spare no effort or
expense to make [itself] an organ of public
opinion, the fearless opponent of oppression
and wrong, the uncompromising advocate of
justice and truth" *Loctn:* Sligo Co Lib (Jan
1849-May 1850); Colin no 1-71 (26 Jan
1849-31 May 1850); NLI (26 Jan 1849-31
May 1850)

A description of the type contents in the
Sligo Guardian or Western Advertiser
from the
Waterloo Directory of Irish Newspapers and Periodicals 1800 - 1900.
- see page 118.

Title: The Champion or Sligo News (continued as Sligo Champion from 1853)
Published in: Sligo, 1836-current
NLI Holdings: 10.1879-in progress (with gaps)
Sligo Co. Library Holdings: 1836-70; 1897-1925
BL Holdings: 6.1836-in progress

LIST OF APPLICANTS

For Registry in the Liberal interest, at Sligo October Quarter Sessions. 1840.

John Francis Blake, house and premises, Ardnaree, barony Tireragh.

Daniel Bree, house and premises, Collooney, barony Tirerill.

James Burns, house and land, Artenelvick, barony Tireragh.

Henry Connor, house and land, Breeogue, barony Carberry.

William Cunningham, house and land, Carrickonelleen, barony Carberry.

Pat. Carty, house and land, Castledargan, barony Tirerill.

Owen Cullenan, house and land, Grange Ormsby, barony Carberry.

Peter Connellan, house and land, Knockaganny, barony Carberry.

Bryan Cunningham, house and land, Loughanelteen, barony Carberry.

William Culkin, houses and land, Farran Morgan, barony Tireragh.

Sir James Crofton, houses and land, Longford, Cloonagh. Carrowble, and Spring Garden, barony Tireragh.

Michael Cunningham, houses and land, Drinaghan, barony Carberry.

Thomas Clark, house and land, Carrowmorris, barony Tireragh.

Pat. Cullinan, house and land, Grange Ormsby, barony Carberry.

Francis Cunningham, house and land, Loughanelteen, barony Carberry.

A list of those applying to be registered as Liberal Voters. from the *Sligo Champion*, October 10th 1840.

We present and appoint the following named persons to form the list of Cesspayers for the respective baronies at the next Special Sessions, to be holden therein, previous to the Summer Assizes, 1851 from which the half first drawn and appearing are to be associated with the Magistrates for the purpose of the Act, 6 & 7 Wm. IV., c. 116sH.

Tireragh	Tirerril
Charles Beatty, Saltport	R. Taylor, Cartron Taylor
Wm. Halliday, Dooneen	John Beatty, Union
Randall Phibbs, Grange	Alexr. Burrows, Drum
Morgan Kilgallon, Grange	Michl. Keogh, Ballinashee
John Christie, Rathlea	John Gethin, Kingsboro
W. Orsmby, Farell McFarell,	Edw. Frazer, Annagh
Thos. McKim, Grangemore	John Donohoe, Cambs
Robt. Wallace, Killeenduff	Richard Gardner, Townhill
Edwd. Williams, Grange	M Thompson, Garoke
T. Kilgallon, Ardnaglass	Wm. Phibbs, Seafield

Corran	Coolavin
J Gorman, Knockshanvalla	R. Elwood, Carroward
Alexe.Duke, Carrickelany	P. McDermot, Rathtarmon
Andw. Green, Cloonlurg	H. Baker, Ardgallon
Robt. Powel, Riversdale	H. Lawrence, Lisserlough
James Knot, Battlefield	E.B. Thornhill, Mt. Irwin
Philip Gemly, Ballymote	S. Shannon, Ardmoyle

List of Cesspayers from the *Sligo Chronicle,* May 1854'.

Title: Sligo Chronicle
Published in: Sligo, 1850-93
Sligo Co. Library Holdings: 4.1850-4.1893

Title: Sligo Independent
Published in: Sligo, 1855-1961
NLI Holdings: 1.1879-12.1961 (with gaps)
Sligo Co. Library Holdings: 9.1855-12.1859 (with gaps)
BL Holdings: 9.1855-7.1869; odd numbers 1870; 1.1875-7.1876; 2-9.1877; 3.1879-9.1921

Title: Sligo Journal
Published in: Sligo, ca. 1807-66
NLI Holdings: 3-12.1823
Sligo Co. Library Holdings: 3-7.1822; 1828-3.1866
BL Holdings: 1.1828-3.1866

Title: Sligo Observer
Published in: Sligo, 1828-31
NLI Holdings: 10.1828-2.1831
Sligo Co. Library Holdings: 10.1828-2.1831
BL Holdings: 10.1828-2.1831

National Newspapers
Through Irish history a range of national newspapers have been published and have ceased publication.These newspapers should also be considered for family history research. Common titles include the *Freeman's Journal, Irish Times* and *Nation*. The increase in the digitising of newspapers makes research more convenient. The main website for some Irish national and local newspapers is Irish Newpaper Archives at www.irishnewsarchive.com/ Also the Irish Times can be searched at www.irishtimes.com/search/

DEATHS FROM STARVATION

The Rev. Mr. Henry, P.P., Bunenadden, county Sligo, in a memorial to the Lord Lieutenant, complained that the following persons met their deaths, by hunger, owing to the neglect of the guardians of the Boyle Union :—

KILSHALVEY ELECTORAL DIVISION.—Mrs. Kilkenny and child—after several applications for relief in vain; Mary Connell, found dead by a rick of turf; Philip M'Gowan's wife and daughter; Bryan Flanagan, found dead by the road side; Widow Davy's daughter; Andrew Davy.

KILTURRA ELECTORAL DIVISION.—John May and son, Pat Marren, Widow Corlely, John O'Hara, John Healy's two daughters. Other deaths from starvation took place previous to my first communication to your excellency not included in this list.

The Lord Lieutenant ordered an inquiry, and the allegations of the Rev. Mr. Henry were most fully proved. The poor law commissioners will, therefore, doubtless remove those personages.

A news item from the *'Nation'* 29th April 1848, page 5.

ADDRESS TO THE RIGHT REV DR. BURKE, ROMAN CATHOLIC BISHOP OF ELPHIN.

WE, the Undersigned Inhabitants of the town and neighbourhood of Sligo, have heard, with extreme regret, that your Lordship has it in contemplation to remove to a different and distant part of your diocese. We sincerely hope that the report is unfounded. A thirty years' residence amongst us has afforded us an opportunity of witnessing the numerous virtues which have marked your conduct in the various relations of social life, and justly endeared your Lordship to all ranks and classes of the community. The urbanity of your manners has won our affections, while the higher and more valuable qualities of your head and heart have engaged our warmest approbation, regard, and esteem. These are the ties which attach us to your Lordship, and we trust they will not now be dissolved by a separation which would give us the deepest and most heartfelt concern. We cannot refrain from again repeating a firm hope that our apprehensions are groundless, and would give expression to our wishes in an earnest request that you will relieve us from our present uneasy state of anxiety and suspense by an assurance that if you ever entertained any idea of removal it is ere now laid aside. A change of residence may, perhaps, throw your Lordship mid a society more agreeable to your taste, and more worthy of your esteem ; but never can your Lordship mingle with any people who will set a higher value on the genuine worth of your character, or more duly appreciate the benefit which society derived from the influence of your truly Christian and exemplary life. We cannot conclude without reminding your Lordship that our request for your continued residence amongst us comes recommended and enforced by the prayers of the poor, whose necessities your kind and constant acts of benevolence have so frequently relieved.

William Phibbs	Robert Faussett
Henry Faucett, J P	Thomas Mostyn
William Parke, D L	Samuel Davidson
Wm Vernon	Thomas Kelly
Richard C Smith	Laurence Vernon, J P
John Ramsay	Stephen M'Creary
David Culbertson	Michael Giblin
Edward M'Lester	Thomas William Neary
Andrew Walsh	Myles Tymrany
D R Palmer	Starky Do…
John Moffott	

It was common for newspapers to publish petitions, which can provide interesting information for the researcher, the above was published in the *Freeman's Journal* 2nd April 1840, p.1

Kilvarnet Parish.

' These epitaphs in Kilvarnet churchyard are given in Dr. O'Rorke's work ' :—

" Hear lys | Interd the Body of BARTH WALLACE | who departed this life the 28th | April 1769. Aged 76."

" Pray for the soul | of OLIVER WALLACE | who departed this | life March 17 1773. | Aged 23 years."

" Pray for the soul of | OWEN DONOGHUE who depart | ed this life March 16th | 1778 aged 60 years. | His son JAMES DONOHOE of Ballyara | his wife JANE BRETT of Tubbercurry and | some of their children are also interred here."

' The following epitaph is placed over the tombstone of the father of the present M.P. for Sligo ' :—

" Lord have mercy on the soul of JOHN COLLEARY of Ranaghan | who departed this life 22 dec. 1841 aged 56. | Erected by his loving wife | MARY MCGRATH. | Requiescant in pace."

" O Lord | have mercy on the | soul of thy servant JOHN | ARMSTRONG of Falnasugan | who departed this life | on 6th of Septr 1843. | aged 74 years. May he rest in | peace. Amen."

" Lord have mercy on the soul of | WILLIAM MASTERSON who departed | this life 12. June. Aged | 96 years. | Erected by his son THOMAS MASTERSON | in memory of him and posterity."

" In | memory of | WILLIAM CORCORAN | Ballinacarrow who departed | this life 16th March 1861. | Aged 43 years. | May he rest in peace."

Kilvarnet parish graveyard inscriptions
extracted from the *Journal of the Association for the Preservation of Memorials of the Dead, Volume 2 (1892-94)*

Chapter 11   Gravestone Inscriptions

Gravestone inscriptions, and other memorials on walls and pews of churches etc., are potentially very useful sources. The information they contain was almost always contributed by the family and therefore usually accurate as regards relationships. They also generally contain the types of information which is treasured by family historians, i.e. names, dates, addresses and relationships. On the other hand, they are not available for all, or even for most. Engraved headstones are expensive items and most people are not commemorated thus. Furthermore, many headstones have weathered or been otherwise damaged, and the inscriptions they bore are no longer visible. Graveyards are also associated with religious denominations, particularly before the 1820s. An interesting account of type and form of Sligo memorials can be found in *"Had me made; a study of the grave memorials of Co. Sligo from c. 1650 to the present"*. Mary B. Timoney. Sligo: TASKS, 2005.

Luckily, the inscriptions from many graveyards have been transcribed and indexed and are available from a range of sources such as local history journals. Particularly valuable sources for Sligo include:

- Transcriptions of 146 graveyards carried out in the 1980s under the aegis of the Co. Sligo Heritage and Genealogical Centre (see page 154). These are in Sligo Library (in 38 volumes referenced as 'Tombstone Inscriptions Co. Sligo') and are indexed by SHGC and accessible as part of their research service.
- The series 'Old Irish Graveyards' published by Kabristan Archives (www.kabristan.org.uk). These five volumes contain almost 4,500 inscriptions abstracted from 40 graveyards by Eileen Hewson.

In addition, Kevin Murray lists inscriptions from a further 16 churches and graveyards on his website http://homepage.eircom.net/~kevm/ Churches.htm. A further generic source is the Journal for the Preservation of Memorials of the Dead (JAPMD) which was published from 1888 until 1937 and included abstracts and inscriptions from all parts of Ireland. The JAPMD content is selective and contributors tended to pick memorials which were of personal interest or otherwise notable. On the positive side, the contributors to the journal sometimes included additional background information on the deceased or the family. The graveyards for which published information is available are listed below. The names are problematic as some cemeteries are ancient and have names which do not match current parish or townland names.

Abbreviations used:

KAB: Kabristan Archives (www.kabristan.org.uk) (see page 136)
SHGC: Sligo Heritage and Genealogical Centre (see page154)
WEB: Partial index on http://homepage.eircom.net/~kevm/Churches.htm
NET: Partial index at www.interment.net

Abbey Graveyard. SHGC (see page 154).
            Achonry RC Church and Communal Graveyard. SHGC
Achonry, St Nathy's and St Brigids C of I. Cathedral. SHGC
Aghanagh Graveyard. FÁS Abstracts indexed by SHGC
Ahamlish Graveyard. FÁS Abstracts indexed by SHGC
Ahamlish Grange. WEB
Aughrish Head near Dromore West: Templeboy Old Graveyard and
      plots. KAB 2.
Aughrish Graveyard. SHGC
Ballinacarrow: Kilvarnet Old Graveyard. KAB 3.
Ballinacarrow Church. SHGC
Ballinafad (Hollybrook) CofI Church and Graveyard. SHGC
Ballinafad RC Church. FÁS Abstracts indexed by SHGC
Ballinafad: Aghanagh Church of Ireland. KAB 5.
Ballaghadereen, St Mary's Graveyard. SHGC
Ballinakill and Sooey. WEB
Ballindoon Abbey Graveyard. SHGC
Ballintogher Church of Ireland. SHGC
Ballintrillick, Keelogues. WEB
Ballintrillick St. Bridgets Church. SHGC
Ballintogher: Killery Burial Ground. KAB1.
Ballintogher: Killery. WEB
Ballintogher, St Teresa's Church. SHGC
Ballisodare: Holy Trinity Church of Ireland. KAB 3.
Old Ballisodare Cemetery. NET

Ballisodare – see also Ballysadare
Ballyara Graveyard. SHGC
Ballygawley: Kilross Burial Ground. KAB1.
Ballygawley, Kilross. WEB
Ballymote RC Church Franciscan Friary Graveyard. KAB3.
Ballymote: Saint Columbas Cemetery. NET
Ballymote Church of Ireland. SHGC
Ballymote RC Church. SHGC
Ballynakill Graveyard. SHGC
Ballyrush RC Church and Graveyard. SHGC
Ballysumaghan Church and Graveyard. SHGC
Ballysadare, Nuns Oratory. SHGC
Ballysadare, Holy Trinity Church of Ireland. SHGC
Ballytivnan, St. Joseph's RC Church. SHGC
Banada Abbey. SHGC
Banada: Corpus Christi Friary burials and churchyard. KAB 3.
Banada Abbey. WEB
Beltra: Dromard Church of Ireland Church of Ireland. KAB 2.
Beltra: Dromard Old Graveyard. KAB 2.
Bunninaden RC Church. SHGC
Calry Church of Ireland. SHGC
Calry: Cloghermore Old Graveyard. KAB 5.
Calry: IGRS Collection, GO
Calry, St Pats Church of Ireland. SHGC
Carrantemple Graveyard, Gurteen. SHGC
Carraroe, St John's Church. SHGC
Carrick (or Carraig) Graveyard. SHGC
Carrigans Ballinfull. WEB
Carrigeens Graveyard Maugherow. SHGC
Carrownanty Graveyard. SHGC
Carrownanty Cemetery. NET
Carrowvard, Dromard Graveyard. SHGC
Castleconnor Church. SHGC
Churchill Graveyard, Dromore West. SHGC
Cippanagh,Templeronan Graveyard. SHGC
Cliffoney Church. SHGC
Clogher Calry. WEB
Clogher, Old Prebyterian Graveyard, Monasteraden. SHGC
Cloghermore Graveyard, Colga. SHGC
Cloonacool Graveyard. SHGC

Sacred to memory
of Joshua Tighe
who exchanged Mortality
for life
10 of June 1859
aged 23 years

Anne C. Graham
Fell asleep in Jesus
4 June 1857
Aged 18 years

James Shaw
of Ballyfaghy
died 9 June·1870
Aged 72 years

Charles William Blyth
son of the late
Lieutenant Charles Blyth R N
died October 6th 1865
Aged 21 years
Jane Blyth widow of the late
Lieutenant Charles Blyth R N
Died Dec 25th 1875

From the *History, Antiquities and Present State of the Parishes of Ballysadare and Kilvarnet in the County of Sligo,*. T O'Rorke (Dublin 1878), which includes 46 Inscriptions

Cloonacool, St. Michaels Church. SHGC
Cloonamahon Church. SHGC
Cloonameehan Graveyard. SHGC
Cloonloo Church. SHGC
Collooney Cemetery. NET
Collooney: St Paul's Church of Ireland. KAB 3.
Collooney Medieval Churchyard. KAB 3.
Collooney, Church of Assumption RC. SHGC
Collooney Abbey. SHGC
Collooney, St Nathy's Graveyard. SHGC
Collooney Methodist Church. SHGC
Collooney, St Paul's CofI, Church and Graveyard. SHGC
Coolaney: Rathbarron Church of Ireland. KAB 4.
Corhawnagh Church, Ballysadare. SHGC
Court Abbey. SHGC
Culfadda RC Church. SHGC
Curry New Graveyard. SHGC
Curry RC Church. SHGC
Curry. WEB
Doo Chapel. SHGC
Dromard Church of Ireland Church and Graveyard. SHGC
Dromard, St Peter's and Paul, RC Church. SHGC
Dromore West: Kilmacshalgan Old Graveyard. KAB 1.
Dromore West Church (new). SHGC
Dromore West Old Church. SHGC
Dromore West, St Mary's Church and Graveyard. SHGC
Drum Methodist Church. SHGC
Drum Presbyterian Church. SHGC
Drumcliff Church and Graveyard. SHGC
Drumcliffe: St. Columba's Cof I (RC and Protestant Burials) KAB 5.
Drumcliffe - The Church of Ireland Parish in its North Sligo Setting.
Stella Durand, Leitrim: Drumlin Publications 2000, ISBN 1 873437 19 6
    (List of surnames. No inscriptions/epitaphs).
Drumcliffe. WEB
Drumcliffe, St. Kevin's Chapel. SHGC
Drumnacillin Graveyard. SHGC
Easkey Abbey Graveyard. SHGC
Easkey Graveyard. SHGC
Easkey RC Church. SHGC
Easky: Roslea Graveyard. KAB 1.

Easky: St. Anne's Church of Ireland. KAB1.
Easky Abbey Graveyard. KAB 1.
Emlaghfad Graveyard. SHGC
Emlaghfad Graveyard. KAB 3.
Enniscrone: Kilglass Church of Ireland. KAB1.
Enniscrone: St. Molaise's Old Cemetery. KAB1.
Enniscrone: Grange Ahamlish Graveyard. KAB 1.
Enniscrone: Killanley Church of Ireland. KAB 3.
Enniscrone: Killanley Old Graveyard Isolated memorials. KAB 3.
Enniscrone Church. SHGC
Enniscrone Graveyard. SHGC
Foyoges Graveyard. SHGC
Friary Church, High St. (Sligo Town). SHGC
Geevagh Church. SHGC
Glen RC Church. SHGC
Glenkilamley. SHGC
Grange Church (Ahamlish). SHGC
Grangemore. SHGC
Gurteen Church of Ireland Graveyard. SHGC
Gurteen: Killaraght Cof I (RC and Protestant burials). KAB 5.
Gurteen Cemetery. NET
Gurteen, St. Patricks RC Church. SHGC
High Wood RC Church. SHGC
Keash: Knockbrack Burial Ground. KAB 4.
Keash RC Church. SHGC
Keelogues Ballintrillick. WEB
Keeloges Graveyard (Glenade). SHGC
Kilanley New Graveyard. SHGC
Kilcummin Cemetery, Cloonacool. Abstract by Orla McCarrick in
    Sligo Library (LIS 068 1998) and on http://www.ancestry.com
Kilcummin Graveyard. SHGC
Kilglass Church and Graveyard. SHGC
Kilglass RC Church. SHGC
Kilglass, St Molaise's Graveyard. SHGC
Killanley Church and Graveyard. SHGC
Killanley Old Graveyard. SHGC
Killaraght Graveyard. SHGC
Killaraght Cemetery. NET
Killaraght, St. Attracta's RC Church. SHGC
Killaspugbrone Graveyard. SHGC

ENNISCRONE
Killanley Church of Ireland

Killanley Church of Ireland built in 1827 is situated about 4 miles south of Enniscrone on the R297, on an unlisted road to the right (coming from Enniscrone). REVD JAMES GREER author of *The Windings of the Moy* is buried here. He was a well-known figure in the locality equipped with a blackthorn stick and a Gladstone bag he would wander the countryside in search of historical material for articles which would later be published in *The Western People* newspaper. He always carried a hip flask to keep out the cold. The graveyard was surveyed by the author in 2008.

ARMSTRONG
> In loving memory of ROBERT ARMSTRONG who died 25th Feb 1894, aged 79 years and of .... (Rest illegible)

ATKINSON
(Draped urn on pillar)
> In memoriam GEORGE ATKINSON ESQ of Ballyshannon, Co.Donegal, departed this life at Ballina, died 5th Feby 1857, aged 65.
> *A weary sufferer at rest in Jesus.*
> *They say He giveth His beloved sleep.*

BOYD
FRONT
> In memoriam GEORGE BOYD MD LRCSI, second son of the late Charles Boyd Esq of Castletown Manor of this Parish who died in New York on the 19th day of July 1872.
> *Jesus said I am the Resurrection and the Life,*
> *He that believeth in Me though he were dead yet shall he live.*
> *And whosoever liveth and believeth in Me shall never die.*

LEFT
> To JOHN eldest and best beloved son died at Castletown Manor, Aug 1st 1868, aged 45 years.
Their MOTHER (no name given) wife of the late Charles Boyd died Dec 30 1894.

BRETT see DUNBARE and BRETT

BRETT see HICKS and BRETT

BURROWS
(Written source)
> JAMES BURROWS died 3rd Nov 1850.

BUTLER
> To the beloved memory of MAJOR WALTER BUTLER son of the late Sir Richard Butler bart of Carryhundon, Co.Carlow, who died on the 14th Decr 1878, aged 76 years.
> *The Lord hath given and the Lord hath taken away.*
> *Blessed be the name of the Lord for ever.*
> *My flesh shall rest in hope.*
> MARIA LOUISA beloved wife of the above died 15th March 1894, aged 89 years. She was the only daughter of Colonel George Jackson of Carramore, Co.Mayo and Sidney Vaughan his wife.

35

Inscriptions from Killanley Church of Ireland
published in
Old Irish Graveyards - County Sligo Part 3
compiled by Eileen Hewson (Kabristan Archives 2009).

Killaville RC Church. SHGC
Killery Graveyard. SHGC
Killery, Ballintogher. WEB
Killoran Graveyard. SHGC
Kilmacowen. WEB
Kilmacowen Graveyard. SHGC
Kilmacshalgan Church of Ireland. KAB 1.
Kilmacshalgan Graveyard. SHGC
Kilmacteige (New Graveyard). SHGC
Kilmacteige Church of Ireland and Graveyard. SHGC
Kilmacteige RC Church. SHGC
Kilmactranny Church and Graveyard. SHGC
New Kilmorgan (Doo). SHGC
Old Kilmorgan Graveyard. SHGC
Kilross Graveyard. SHGC
Kilshalvey Graveyard. SHGC
Kilturra Graveyard. SHGC
Kiltyclogher Graveyard. SHGC
Kilvarnet Graveyard. SHGC
Knockbrack Graveyard, Culfadda. SHGC
Knockmore Abbey, Mount Irwin Graveyard. SHGC
Knocky Graveyard, Ballysadare. SHGC
Largan Church (Kilmacteige). SHGC
Lavagh Church. SHGC
Lissadell Church and Graveyard. SHGC
Lisadell. WEB
Maugherow: Lissadell Church of Ireland. KAB 5.
Maugherow: Carrigans Cemetery. KAB 5.
Maugherow, St. Patricks Church. SHGC
Monasteraden Graveyard. SHGC
Monasteraden RC Church. SHGC
Moylough Church (Curry). SHGC
Mullaghmore: Nun's Oratory. SHGC
Ransboro Old Church. SHGC
Ransboro, Our Lady Star of the Sea. SHGC
Rathbarren Church of Ireland and Graveyard. SHGC
Rathcormack R.C. Church. SHGC
Rathlee Church. SHGC
Rhue Graveyard, Tubbercurry. SHGC
Riverstown Church Of Ireland. SHGC

200

" Laborions blast on Neptune's waves has tossed me to and fro,
But spite of all, by God's decree, I harbour here below ;
And now at anchor here I lie with many of our fleet,
I hope to sail some day again our Saviour Christ to meet."

These lines appear to be an attempt to repeat those given on page 237, vol. i., and on page 62 of this vol.

Parish of Kilturra.

'The Very Rev. Dr. O'Rorke, M.R.I.A., in the " History of Sligo, Town and County," vol. ii., page 195, gives a very exhaustive and graphic description of this parish, which is partly situated in the Counties of Mayo and Sligo. The old churchyard is in Sligo, on the townland of Kilturra, and within Mr. Cooke's demesne. It is well fenced and kept, and a nice road leads up to the entrance gate. Though undoubtedly a very ancient burial-place, It contains no tombs of an earlier date than 1771. It may be right to say that there are some peculiar customs and some immunities attached to this graveyard worthy of mention.

'It is the custom, which dates from time immemorial, not to open a grave in Kilturra on a Friday ; whilst rats, though swarming in thousands in the river near by, have not been seen within the graveyard since a good bishop (" I tell the tale as it was told to me "), who resided here in the last century, blessed it, and like St. Patrick, with other vermin, " banished them for ever."

'The tombs of most interest are those of the Cooke and Irwin families.

'The Cookes rest in a slightly-raised mound enclosed by iron-railing and planted with some yews and other evergreens, and at the head of the graves there stands a stately Celtic Cross, with the crest (an ostrich holding a horseshoe in his bill) incised on the shaft, and on a white marble slab on pedestal, the following inscription is carved ' :—

" Thomas Cooke, esquire, | who departed this life
September 1st, 1879. Aged 70 years. | William, his son,
October 24th, 1874. Aged 18 years. | Elizabeth, his
dau., June 29th, 1878. Aged 21 years. | Eleanor, his
dau., January 28th, 1881. Aged 19 years."

'The oldest epitaph in the place is inscribed on a plain upright stone, in roughly-cut capital letters, as follows. (This headstone faces the west, but this was the entrance to the vault in which the family were interred, while all the others in the graveyard are faced to the east) :—

" HERE LIES THE BODY OF | MR. ALEXANDER
IRWIN who | departed this life in the |
YEAR 1761. AND his wife ISMAY | IRWIN
ALIAS KELLY and their posterity. THIS
TOMB | WAS ERECTED BY HIS THIRD | SON
DOCTOR THOMAS IRWIN the year 1771."

An extract from the *Journal of the Association for the Preservation of Memorials of the Dead, Volume 2 (1892-94).*

Riverstown RC Church. SHGC
Riverstown: Church of the Sacred Heart. KAB 4.
Riverstown (Sooey): Saint Joseph Cemetery. NET
Rockfield Church, Coolaney. SHGC
Rockfield Graveyard. SHGC
Rosses Point Cofl. SHGC
Rosses Point Graveyard. SHGC
Rosses Point. WEB
Rosses Point, St. Columba's Church. SHGC
Scarden, Strandhill. WEB
Scarden Graveyard, Strandhill. SHGC
Skreen Church and Graveyard. SHGC
Skreen RC Church. SHGC
Skreen Church of Ireland (RC and Protestant burials). KAB 2.
Skreen, St Mary's Graveyard. SHGC
Sligo Abbey: IGRS Collection NLI
Sligo Town: Holy Cross Abbey Sligo Gaol Executions Isolated
    memorials. KAB 4.
Strandhill: St. Anne's Church of Ireland. KAB 2.
Sligo, St John's (C.of I): Church and Parish of St. John, Tyndall,
    Ir.2741p 20; also in Brian J. Cantwell's Memorials of the Dead: The
    Collected Works. Available on www.findmypast.ie
Sligo City Cemetery. Register of Internment (1) 1851-1920; (2) 1920-
    2004 and Death Register (3) 1855-1931 and (4) 1855-1931. Pub.
    Sligo Borough Council (2005). Available in Sligo Public Library
    and indexed by SHGC.
Sligo: Cathedral of Immaculate Conception. SHGC
Sligo: Mercy Convent Graveyard (Sligo Town). SHGC
Sligo: Methodist Church, Wine St. (Sligo Town). SHGC
Sligo: Nazareth Convent Graveyard (Sligo Town). SHGC
Sligo: Presbyterian Church. SHGC
Sligo Abbey Graveyard (Sligo Town). SHGC
Sligo City Cemetery (Sligo Town). SHGC
St. Anne's Cofl Graveyard. SHGC
Sligo: St. Anne's Church (Sligo Town). SHGC
Sligo: St. John's Cathedral and Graveyard (Sligo Town). SHGC
Sligo: Ursuline Convent Graveyard. SHGC
Sooey and Ballinakill. WEB
Sooey Church. SHGC

Sooey Graveyard. SHGC
Strandhill, Scarden. WEB
Strandhill, St. Anne's Church and Graveyard. SHGC
Strandhill, St Pat's. Church. SHGC
Taunagh Church of Ireland. KAB 4.
Tawnagh Graveyard Riverstown War Casualties. KAB4.
Tawnagh Graveyard. SHGC
Templeboy RC Church. SHGC
Templeboy: Grangemore Graveyard and family plots and Isolated
   memorials. KAB 2.

SLIGO CEMETERY

Old Section

Compiled by EILEEN HEWSON

Kabristan Archives

Wem

Over 5,700 memorial inscriptions of County Sligo,
compiled by Eileen Hewson
and published by *Kabristan Archives* - see page 136

Templeboy Old Graveyard. (Aughrish Head near Dromore W.) KAB 2.
Templeboy, St. Joseph's Graveyard. SHGC
Templemore Graveyard. SHGC
Templeronan Cemetery. NET
Thurlestrane. WEB
Templevanney Graveyard. SHGC
Tourlestrane, St. Attracta's RC Church. SHGC
Tubbercurry Church and Graveyard. SHGC
Tubbercurry: St. George's Church of Ireland Isolated graves. KAB 5.
Tubbercurry, St. John's RC Church. SHGC

Kabristan Publications

Kabristan Publications have produced many books related to memorial inscriptions in Ireland and abroad. Their catalogue includes inscriptions for Sligo's neighbouring counties, Mayo and Leitrim. Their *'Old Irish Graveyards County Sligo'* by Eileen Hewson are available in six volumes:

Part 1: (10 graveyards index of approx 850 memorials
ISBN 978-1-906276-29-4)
Part 2: (6 graveyards index of approx 870 memorials
ISBN 978-1-906276-30-0)
Part 3: (9 graveyards index of 930 memorials
ISBN 978-1-906276-31-7)
Part 4: (8 graveyards index of approx 766 memorials
ISBN 978-1-906276-32-4)
Part 5: (7 graveyards index of approx 1007 memorials
ISBN 978-1-906276-33-1)
also:
Sligo Cemetery Old Section: see page 136.
For further details visit: www.genealogybookshop.co.uk/

Chapter 12

Further Reading and Miscellaneous Sources

Included in this chapter are a wide variety of publications which will assist your research in one of several ways. Firstly, the evidence which your ancestors left is determined by local events and organisations, and by local practices and customs. Awareness of local history and culture may reveal useful sources of information. This list therefore includes local histories of Sligo towns, parishes and associations. It also contains publications describing the involvement of Sligo people in national and international events. Some of these publications are self-published or privately printed (indicated as Pr.pr.) and rare. However, they are increasingly becoming available in digital format. A web search may be useful in finding a digital copy to access, or a copy from a book-seller.

Titles below which are followed by the symbol **W** can be downloaded free from www.askaboutireland.ie

General Reading

Hall *Mr. and Mrs.*	*Sligo. 'Ireland- Its Scenery, Character etc.* (London 1843) Vol.III pp.306-320.
Hayes-McCoy, *G.A.*	*Index to The Compossicion Booke of Connoght.* Irish Manuscripts Commission Dublin, NL Ir. 412 c 1
Kilgannon, *Tadhg*	*Sligo and its surroundings; a descriptive and pictorial guide to the history, scenery, antiquities, and places of interest in and around Sligo.* Sligo: Kilgannon and sons, Ltd., 1926. Reprint, Sligo, 1988, Dodd's Antiquarian Books
McCormack, *Gareth*	*Portrait of County Sligo.* Wellington: Halsgrove, 2010

SLIGO.

THE maritime county of Sligo, in the province of Connaught, is bounded on the east by the county of Leitrim, on the north by the Atlantic ocean, on the west and south by Mayo county, and on the south-east by the county of Roscommon. It comprises an area of 434,188 statute acres; 257,217 of which are cultivated; 168,711 are unimproved mountain and bog; and 8260 are under water. Its population was in 1821, 146,229; and in 1831, amounted to 171,508. It is divided into six baronies—Carbery, Coolavin, Corran, Leney, Tiraghrill, and Tyreragh. Its principal towns are the assize town of Sligo, Ballymote, and Collooney.

The town of Sligo is a sea-port, but its trade is very limited, although it is the only port of much importance upon the western coast between London-

derry and Galway. Its abbey has been long famous; and its ruins are classed among the most remarkable in Ireland. The abbey was founded in 1257, by Maurice Fitzgerald, Earl of Kildare and Lord Justice. In 1270,

A page from
'Ireland- Its Scenery, Character etc.' by Mr. and Mrs. S.C. Hall
(London 1843)
- see page 137.

McTernan,
John C.

Olde Sligoe: aspects of town and county over 750 years.
Sligo: Avena Publications, 1995

Memory harbour: the Port of Sligo: an outline of its growth and decline and its role as an emigration port.
Sligo: Avena Publications 1992.

In Sligo long ago: Aspects of town and country over two centuries.
Sligo: Avena Press, 1998.

Sligo sources of local history: a catalogue of the local history collection, with an introduction and guide to sources.
Sligo County Library, 1988.

Historic Sligo: A Bibliographical Introduction to the Antiquities and History of Co. Sligo.
1965.

Sligo G.A.A.: a centenary history, 1884-1984.
Sligo: [GAA] Coiste Chontae Shligigh, 1984.

McGowan,
J.

A Bitter Wind.
Aeolus Publications 2009. (Local folklore and customs).

Sligo: Land of Destiny.
Sligo: Cottage Publications 2004.

Echoes of a Savage Land.
Cork: Mercier Press 2001. (Local folklore and customs).

O'Dowd,
Mary

Power, politics and land: early modern Sligo 1568-1688.
Belfast Institute of Irish Studies, Queen's University of Belfast 1991

were often impounded for rent, even when the balance for labour was in their favour.

When at home and at work, the labourers are generally clothed very insufficiently; and many of those who possess a good suit, do not wear it except on Sundays and on particular occasions. The women and children, especially the latter, are still worse off than the men. The children indeed are constantly in rags.

None of the cabins visited by the Assistant Commissioners had ceilings; and the dirt and cobwebs that were continually falling from the roof was a serious inconvenience in a district devoted to the making of butter for exportation. Most of the miserable huts contained rude bedsteads, but very frequently no other bedding than straw or hay, and a single quilt or sheet, made of coarse sacking, invariably in a condition of great filth. When the family was a large one, the bedsteads were occupied by the parents and the younger children, the others having nothing but a litter of old hay, which, in the day time, was collected in a heap in a corner, and had in most

A page from *'The Miseries and Beauties of Ireland' Vol.I*
by Jonathan Binns (London 1837).

O'Flanagan, **Michael**	*Sligeach.* Dublin 1944
O'Rorke, **Rev. T**	*History of Sligo, town and county.* Dublin 1889 (Reprint, Sligo, 1986, Dodd's Antiquarian Books).
	History, antiquities, and present state of the parishes of Ballysadare and Kilvarnet, in the county of Sligo; with notices of the O'Haras, the Coopers, the Percivals, and other local families. Dublin 1878. J Duffy and Sons.
Simms, **J. G.**	*County Sligo in the 18th century.* The Journal of the Royal Society of Antiquaries of Ireland, Vol. XCI, pt. 2, pp. 153-162, 1961.

Of the Protestant landowners at the beginning of the eighteenth century the most remarkable were the O'Haras, who were distinguished by their Gaelic name and descent from the Coopers, Gores, Ormsbys, Joneses, Irwins and other landed families of the county. The O'Haras were a relic of the ancient proprietors, a distinction they owed to the fact that early in the seventeenth century Teigue O'Hara had died leaving two minor sons who were put in charge of the court of wards[3] and brought up as Protestants. But they were not bigoted Protestants; they had many Catholic relatives and Kean O'Hara who owned Annaghmore at the beginning of the eighteenth century married a wife from a well-known Catholic family, the Mathews of Thomastown, County Tipperary. Kean O'Hara was on very friendly terms with Counsellor MacDonagh. The O'Haras also gave shelter to the Catholic bishop of Achonry in his distress.[4]

An extract from *'County Sligo in the 18th century'* - see above

Sligo County Council	*Milestones and memories; Sligo County Council centenary record: 1899 - 1999.* Sligo: Sligo County Council, 2000? NLI 3B 1048
Co. Sligo Famine Commemoration Committee	*Co. Sligo Famine Book.* 1997.

Wood-Martin, W.G. *History of Sligo county and town: From the close of the revolution of 1688 to the present time.* Wood-Martin, W.G. Dublin: Hodges, Figgis and Co., 1892. **W**

History of Sligo county and town: From the accession of James I to the revolution of 1688. Dublin: Hodges, Figgis and Co., 1889. Reprint, Sligo, 1990, Dodd's Antiquarian Books. **W**

History of Sligo county and town: From the earliest ages to the close of the reign of Queen Elizabeth. Dublin: Hodges, Figgis and Co., 1882. Reprint, Sligo, 1990, Dodd's Antiquarian Books. **W**

Sligo and the Enniskilleners. From 1688-1691. Dublin, Hodges, Figgis, 1880.

Local Histories

Achonry see Killala
see Tuam

Ardagh Monahan, Rev. J
Records Relating to the Diocese of Ardagh and Clonmacnoise.
1886

Ballymote Rogers, Nuala
Ballymote: aspects through time.
Sligo, privately published 1994.

McDonagh, J.C.
History of Ballymote and the parish of Emlaghfad. Dublin. 1936, NL Ir. 94122 m 1

Benada Butler, Katherine
The story of Benada.
pr.pr. 1982

Benbulben	*In the Shadow of Benbulben: History and folklore of Sligo's Yeats Country.* Aeolus 1993. Reprinted and updated 1994 and 2000.ISBN: 0952133407
Charlestown	Morris, Morgan. *Charlestown and its surroundings.* Sligo: Blackwood, 1988.
Enniscrone	Mac Hale, C *Enniscrone, Co.Sligo.* 1989.
Castleconnor	*Castleconnor parish: an historical perspective pre 1900.* Sligo: Castleconnor Parish Development Group, 2000.
Cillglas	Carroll, P.J. *Cillglas - Kilglas: the church by the stream: a history of the confiscation settlement and vesting of its lands.* Pr.pr. 1996.
Collooney	see also: Killoran McGarry, Jim *Collooney* Boyle 1980
Coolera	McTernan, John C. *At the foot of Knocknarea: a chronicle of Coolera in bygone days.* Sligo: Coolera/Strandhill G.A.A., 1990.
Dromard	see Skreen
Elphin	*The diocese of Elphin: people, places and pilgrimage.* Dublin: Columba Press, 2000.
Emlaghfad	see Ballymote

Geevagh	McGloin, Atlanta and Moore, Sam (eds) *Aspects of Geevagh and Highwood, County Sligo.* Geevagh, Co. Sligo. Geevagh Redevelopment Association 1996
Gleann	*In the shadow of Carran Hill: historical perspectives of Gleann and its surroundings* [S.l.]: [s.n.], 1997.
Gurteen	Finn, J. *Gurteen, Co. Sligo, Its history and antiquities and traditions.* 1981, NL Ir. 94122 p1
Inishcrone	Mac Hale, Conor *Inishcrone and O'Dubhda Country: Inis Crabhann agus Dúiche Uí Dhubhda* by. Dublin: IHR Publications, 2003.
Inishmurray	McGowan, Joe. *Inishmurray: gale, stone and fire: portrait of a fabled island.* Mullaghmore. Co. Sligo: Aeolus, 1998. McGowan, J. *Inishmurray: Island Voices,* (History and folklore of Inishmurray island). Aeolus Publications 2004 ISBN 0 952133423
Killala	Miriam Moffitt *The Church of Ireland community of Killala and Achonry, 1870-1940* Dublin; Portland, or: Irish Academic Press, 1999. ISBN: 0716526824 (pbk.) **see also Tuam**
Killoran	Farry, Michael *Killoran and Coolaney: A local History.* Killoran Press, Trim 1985.

Riverstown   Jack Johnston
The Riverstown story; County Sligo.
[Sligo]: [Riverstown Enterprise Development],
[2005] NLI 5B 1609

Rosses Point   Scholastica, S. M.
In and around Rosses Point, Sligo.
The Irish Monthly, Feb., 1912, pp. 61-69; Mar.,
1912, pp. 124-134 ;Apr., 1912, pp. 217-225

---

withstood the ravages of time and of the ruthless invader. The
Abbey was attacked in 1642 by the infamous Sir Frederick
Hamilton, of Manorhamilton, a Parliamentarian soldier, who
wantonly set fire to it and murdered those of the friars who
tried to escape. The story goes—it is one of those

> legends writ in blood
> That shoot across time's thunderous flood.
> The earnest, sinewy Irish story
> Lit with our Faith's unfading glory.

It relates that when one of Hamilton's regiments was leaving
the burning town, not knowing the locality, the captain of the
corps seized a man named M'Sharry, and forced him to act as
guide to these devil's agents, and in order to be able to see
M'Sharry in the dark they bade him put on the white habit of
one of the murdered friars. Now, this M'Sharry was a nimble
mountaineer who knew every spot of the locality for miles around.
He led them " o'er moor and fen, o'er crag and torrent," through
ragged woods and stony mountain paths, till the burning abbey
behind them seemed but a mere glow in the western sky. At
last, when they reached the top of Cope's Mountain, a glimmering
of light began to dawn on the mind of the obtuse English captain,
and he imperiously demanded of the simple-looking guide whither
he was leading them. " To your father, the devil," came the
unexpected reply, and with that M'Sharry disappeared over the
edge of the chasm, and Hamilton's troopers shot after him into
space, and went crashing down into the depths of Lugnagall
(" the foreigner's abyss ") ; but M'Sharry clung to a sapling at
the verge of the cliff, and listened delightedly to the Sassenachs
hurtling into the depths below on their way, as we may be sure
he told himself, to the still deeper depths of Avernus. " But
the pity of it was," the local car-drivers will add with sly humour
" the pity of it was the devil didn't then get his own playboy,
Sir Frederick, before he had time to do more mischief." This

From *'In and around Rosses Point, Sligo'*
- see above.

Skreen	Michael O'Horo. *Skreen and Dromard: history and heritage'*. Skreen, Co. Sligo: Pr.pr. 2000.

Roy Clements
Mainly Skreen and Dromard in Co Sligo.
Pub: Dari Press, 2005. NLI 5A 2847

Sligo (town) Gallagher, Fióna
The streets of Sligo: urban evolution over the course of seven centuries.
Sligo: the author, 2008 ISBN: 9780955806100

Tuam Knox, H.T.
Notes on the Early History of the Dioceses of Tuam, Killala, and Achonry.
Dublin 1904

Miscellaneous Publications and Articles

Deignan, Padraig *The Protestant community in Sligo, 1914-49.*
Dublin: Original Writing, 2010.

Farry, Michael *Sligo 1914-1921: a chronicle of conflict.*
Killoran Press, Trim 1992. ISBN: 0952013509

Fleming, D. A. *Politics and provincial people: Sligo and Limerick, 1691-1761.* Manchester: Manchester University Press, c2010. TCD 320.9415 R0

Moran, Gerard P *Sir Robert Gore Booth and his landed estate in County Sligo, 1814-1876: land, famine, emigration and politics.* Dublin: Four Courts Press, 2006.

Hamilton, Michael *Down memory line; the Sligo Leitrim and Northern Counties Railway.* Manorhamilton, Co. Leitrim: Drumlin Publications, 1997.

In the eighteenth century Sligo was a remote and seldom visited part of Ireland. It was far from Dublin and not on the way to anywhere else, except from Donegal to Mayo. Right up to the end of the century there was no mail-coach route from Dublin to Sligo. There was only one town, and for much of the period it was small and undeveloped. The county had no resident nobility, not even a bishop's palace. Until 1798 life was uneventful and Sligo finds little mention in the general history of eighteenth-century Ireland. But the local history for the period is well documented and there is a variety of sources, printed and unprinted, from which we can form a picture of a self-contained society with an individual way of living that has many points of interest.

Social and economic conditions in eighteenth-century Ireland were to a great extent the result of the wars of the seventeenth century in which the Protestants, first in Cromwell's time and then in William of Orange's, defeated the Catholics and as a result got nearly all the land and enjoyed a complete monopoly of political and administrative power. Sligo is, of course, part of Connacht, and was so in Cromwell's time. But it was not part of the Connacht reserved for the Irish under the transplantation scheme; it was earmarked for Cromwell's soldiers. At the restoration of Charles II some Catholics got back part of the lands that Cromwell had taken from them. But some got nothing back and among these were O'Connor Sligo and O'Gara, who had owned a great part of the county. The only prominent Catholic landowner in the county to be restored was Lord Taafe, who got back his estates at Ballymote. Less than ten per cent of the county was owned by Catholics at the end of Charles II's reign.

A description of Sligo from
'County Sligo in the 18th century'
- see page 141.

IISQUB, *RIA*	*Counties of South Ulster, 1834-8: Cavan, Leitrim, Louth, Monaghan and Sligo.* Belfast: Institute of Irish Studies in association with the Royal Irish Academy, 1998.
INTO	*The national schools of County Sligo [1931-1999].* Irish National Teachers' Organisation. County Sligo INTO Millennium Committee. Sligo: Highwood Community Resource Centre, 1999.
Jackson *R. W. Arthur.*	*Freemasonry in Sligo 1767 to 1867.* Pub: Beverley: Wright and Hoggard, 1909. NLI 1B 2324
	Freemasonry in Sligo 1767 to 1867. Pub: Beverley: Wright and Hoggard, 1909. NLI 1B 2324
M'Parlan. *James*	*Statistical survey of the county of Sligo, with observations on the means of improvement; drawn up in the year 1801, for the consideration, and under the direction of the Dublin Society.* Royal Dublin Society. Dublin, printed by Graisberry and Campbell, 1802. **W**
McTernan *John C.*	*A Sligo miscellany; a chronicle of people, places and events of other days.* Sligo, Avena Publications, 2000.
	Historic Sligo: a bibliographical introduction to the antiquities and history.and notable individuals. Sligo: Yeats Co. Publications, 1965.
NAI Ms	*Records of the Sligo Militia 1855-1857.* NAI M2558-63.
Sprinks *Neil*	*Sligo, Leitrim and Northern Counties Railway.* Published: Hassocks, Sussex: Irish Railway Record Society [London Area], 1981
Sligo Champion	*The Sligo Champion sesquicentenary 1836-1986.* Sligo Champion, 1986

Chapter 13   Archive and Internet Information

As explained in the introduction, the records which you will need to access for your Sligo research are located in several different archives. Although many of these are now accessible on-line, some are still only available from these repositories. Below is a listing of the major archives (all of which have websites), and also other websites of value to your search.

Major Archives:

General Register Office, (GRO)
www.groireland.ie
This is the central repository for birth, death and marriage records. Details of records available, costs, and access information on the website above. The headquarters is located in Roscommon (Tel: +353 (0) 90 6632900 LoCall: 1890 252076) but a research facility is available at: 3rd Floor, Block 7, Irish Life Centre, Lower Abbey Street, Dublin 1.

National Archives of Ireland (NAI),
Bishop Street, Dublin 8.
www.nationalarchives.ie
The NAI houses a vast collection of relevant records generated by public bodies (censuses, wills, and other government records etc). It also provides a free professional genealogical advisory service. It is necessary to obtain a readers ticket to access the records, but this can be done on-site. The website is very user-friendly and it is advisable to order items in advance as some material is stored off-site.

National Library of Ireland (NLI),
Kildare Street,
Dublin 2
www.nli.ie
The NLI is another major repository and its holdings are mainly those generated by non-government organisations or individuals (Books, newspapers, estate papers etc). It also contains a major collection of microfilmed Catholic Church registers. It also has a dedicated free genealogical service. Contact with the NLI can be made at Tel. (01) 6618811 and at www.nli.ie

Registry of Deeds,
Henrietta Street,
Dublin 1
www.landregistry.ie
The Registry of Deeds holds deeds dating back to 1708. In the same building is the Land Registry, which has land records since 1892. Its website is a good introduction to the indexation and documentation on hand.

Representative Church Body Library (RCBL)
Braemor Park,
Churchtown,
Dublin 14.
www.library.ireland.anglican.org
Archives of Church of Ireland records, mainly from the Republic of Ireland including records of over 1,000 parishes. Also records of societies and organisations related to the church.

Valuation Office,
Irish Life Centre,
Abbey Street Lower,
Dublin 1.
www.valoff.ie
The Valuation Office holds the valuation records of all Irish properties from 1846 as well as valuation maps from c.1850. Its basis is Griffith's Valuation and changes in land occupancy for each holding can be tracked from its records.

Major Websites:
The websites of the above archives are hugely valuable sources. In addition, however there are other websites of value.

1901 and 1911 Census
www.censusnationalarchives.ie
This excellent site is run by the National Archives above and provides free access to the 1901 and 1911 census data.

www.askaboutireland.ie
This is run by the Library Council of Ireland and is largely aimed at schools. However, it provides access to Griffith's Valuation, to many maps, and also downloads of local histories.

www.irishgenealogy.ie
This government site is a portal to some of the other national websites, but also provides a free search facility for church records in parts of Dublin, Kerry, Carlow and Cork. Addition of further records to the site is planned.

www.rootsireland.ie
This site is run by the IFHF (see page 152) which runs a network of local county Heritage or genealogy centres which have indexed local church records. The site provides central access to the records of these Heritage centres. Existence of a record can be established free on the site, but a fee will be charged for access to the details.

www.findmypast.ie
This site provides subscription-based access to Prison records (1790-1924); the order books of the Petty Sessions (i.e. a local court for minor cases) from 1850-1910; and a range of other sources (directories, military sources etc.).

www.rootsweb.ancestry.com/~irlsli/sligocountyireland.html.
This excellent site has a range of materials donated by volunteers including transcriptions of church and other records and a forum for Sligo researchers.

http://sources.nli.ie/
A database of manuscripts and articles of Irish relevance in the National Library and in many other archives in Ireland and elsewhere. It is worth a search for the area in which you are interested.

www.familysearch.org
This is the site of the Mormon Church, or Church of Jesus Christ of Latter-day Saints whose Salt Lake City headquarters houses the largest library of genealogical information in the world. Mormon churches usually have a family history section and welcome researchers.

In addition to the above specialist Irish sites, other international websites (Ancestry.com; familysearch.org etc.) will also contain many Irish records.

Local Repositories and Organisations:

The Irish Family History Foundation
The Irish Family History Foundation runs the Irish Genealogical Project which has a nationwide network of genealogical centres, each of which has indexed local records and provides genealogical research services. Their website www.rootsireland.ie is described above.
The local centre in Sligo is:

County Sligo Heritage and Genealogy Centre
www.sligoroots.com/
Aras Reddan,
Temple Street,
Sligo.
Tel: 00353 (0)71 9143728
Email: info@sligoroots.com
see also page 154.

Sligo County Library
http://www.sligolibrary.ie
Sligo Library Headquarters,
Stephen Street,
Sligo.
Ph. 071 9111850
A major repository of material on Sligo history and culture. The local history section is open to visitors, but it may be wise to make arrangements in advance as research space is limited and actively used.

Societies and Sources:

Association of Professional Genealogists in Ireland.
www.apgi.ie
The accredited organisation of genealogists available to conduct research on your behalf.

Genealogical Society of Ireland.
www.familyhistory.ie
Members interested in Irish genealogy; publishes the Genealogical Society of Ireland journal.

Irish Family History Society.
www.ifhs.ie
Also accepts members and publishes an annual journal and news-sheets.

Sligo Field Club
www.sligofieldclub.ie/
A membership based organisation which promotes interest in all aspects of Sligo's past, including genealogy and local history.

Irish Roots Magazine.
www.irishrootsmagazine.com
A quarterly magazine dedicated to Irish genealogy

Garda Archives (Police).
Contains much data, including documents and photographs, on police history going back before the establishing of the Irish Garda in 1922. Tel. (01) 6669998 and www.garda.ie/angarda/museum.html

County Sligo Heritage & Genealogy Centre
Aras Reddan, Temple Street, Sligo, Ireland

County Sligo Heritage & Genealogy Society was established in 1988. It is a community owned company set up to identify, collect, record and computerise documentary and genealogical information relating to County Sligo. The Society established County Sligo Heritage and Genealogy Centre, which has been providing a comprehensive research service to people tracing their County Sligo roots for over 25 years. The centre offers an extensive range of services and products to both individuals and special interest groups.

Genealogical Research Services
• Single record search
• Family search
• Family history report
• Online research

Visitor Services
• Research consultation service
• Location search
• Same day research service

Community Heritage Events
• Clan gatherings
• Genealogy festivals
• Community information workshops

The centre is part of a national network of designated genealogical resaearch centres in Ireland and is a member of the Irish family history foundation. It is a non-profit enterprise partially funded by POBAL under their Community Services Programme. All monies accrued from its operations are used to maintain the provision of the service.

Location
The County Sligo Heritage & Genealogy Centre is located in the Regional Tourism Headquarters at Temple Street in Sligo.

Contact Details
Website:: www.sligoroots.com
Email: info@sligoroots.com
Telephone: +353 71 914 3728

government supporting communities

An Roinn Coimirce Sóisialaí
Department of Social Protection
www.welfare.ie

Index

CERTIFICATE OF CONFORMITY.

Arthur, by Divine Providence, Lord Archbishop of Dublin, Primate and Metropolitan of Ireland; To all whom these presents may concern, GREETING.

We do hereby certify, That Hyacinth O'Rorke, Now of Dublin, hath renounced the errors of the Church of Rome; and was by our order received into the Communion of the Church of Ireland, on Thursday the 12th inst. November. And that the said Hyacinth O'Rorke is a Protestant, and doth conform to the Church of Ireland, as by Law established. In witness whereof We have caused our Manual Seal to be affixed to these presents this Twelfth Day of November 1767.

Arth. Dublin.

[Seal]

DUBLIN; Printed by *Boulter Grierson, Printer to the King's Most Excellent Majesty*, MDCCLXVII.

---

from '*History, antiquities, and present state of the parishes of Ballysadare and Kilvarnet, in the county of Sligo; with notices of the O'Haras...*'
-see page 141

Sept 2012